AF600631

Requisites of Intention in the Reception of the Sacraments

THE CATHOLIC UNIVERSITY OF AMERICA
CANON LAW STUDIES
No. 391

Requisites of Intention in the Reception of the Sacraments

A DISSERTATION

Submitted to the Faculty of the School of Canon Law of the Catholic University of America in Partial Fulfillment of the Requirements for the Degree of the Doctorate in Canon Law

BY

REVEREND LEO V. VANYO, J.C.L.
Priest of the Diocese of Pittsburgh

THE CATHOLIC UNIVERSITY OF AMERICA
WASHINGTON, D. C.
1965

Nihil Obstat:

CLEMENT BASTNAGEL
Censor Deputatus

May 12, 1961

Imprimatur:

✠ JOHN J. WRIGHT
Bishop of Pittsburgh

May 24, 1961

Printed by
THE WICKERSHAM PRINTING COMPANY
Lancaster, Pennsylvania

FOREWORD

Our Lord instituted the seven sacraments to serve as so many channels through which grace was to be transmitted to men. They were to be most important, sometimes most necessary, means for salvation.

Their administration Christ committed to His Church. The ordinary ministers of these sacraments were, except in the case of matrimony, men specially deputed for this task by the Church. In their office these men were to function as ministers of Christ, acting in His name, freely and deliberately.

In regard to matters of salvation God never forces the human will. It is rather allowed to remain free to choose as it wishes. Therefore, the Church too has insisted that the sacraments, despite their very great importance, are to be ministered only to those who freely request them.

Simple freedom, however, was not considered to be sufficient. Accordingly the Church declared that a positive act of the will, a positive intention, was necessary, both for the minister of the sacraments as well as for the recipient. Authors then sought to determine what kind of intention would indeed be required but would also suffice for the valid reception of the sacraments.

Because of the complexity of the problem of matrimonial consent, and also in view of its uniqueness, it has been considered best to treat here solely of the intention that is required in the first six sacraments to the exclusion of what relates to the sacrament of matrimony.

The writer wishes here to express his gratitude to the Faculty of the School of Canon Law of the Catholic University of America for their guidance and direction in the writing of this dissertation, and to all others who have in any way contributed to its preparation.

TABLE OF CONTENTS

PAGE

CHAPTER III

CHAPTER IV

CHAPTER V

CHAPTER I

THE INTENTION IS DIVIDED AND CONSIDERED UNDER A THREEFOLD ASPECT

A. Concept of Intention in General

In his division of human acts, St. Thomas (1225-1274) placed intention among those acts which proceed from the will. "It appears," he said, "that there are three acts of the will in reference to the end: viz., volition, fruition and intention."[1]

The proper object of the will is the "good," whether this be a true good, or only an apparent good, the *"bonum apparens."* The will, then, is moved toward the good as towards its end. It is moved first of all toward the universal good. In fact, however, experience shows that it finds itself in its daily activity in the presence of many particular goods. Toward some of these particular goods the will proceeds no further than to a simple willing or wishing of these goods, what later Latin writers call *"simplex volitio boni."* If, however, the object of the act of the will is not simply a wish, but the act of the will includes as well the means which are necessary or useful for attaining that object, then there is present a true intention. The fundamental distinction, then, between the simple willing and an intention lies in this that "velle tendit in finem absolute; intendere autem appetit finem per media apte ordinata."[2]

St. Thomas used the example of health, which can be a good which is simply desired, or which is truly intended, whenever the will includes those means which will be necessary to acquire it.

> Intention is an act of the will in regard to the end. . . . It considers the end as the term toward which something is

[1] "Actus autem voluntatis in finem videntur esse tres; scilicet velle, frui, et intendere."—St. Thomas Aquinas, *Summa Theologica* (Matriti: Biblioteca de Autores Cristianos, 1952), Pars Ia-IIae, q. 8.

[2] Cappello, *De Sacramentis,* Vol. I (5. ed., Romae: Marietti, 1947), n. 38.

> ordained; and thus intention regards the end. For when we speak of intending to have health, we mean not only that we will to have it, but that we will to have it by means of something else.[3]

Thus, the sick man suffering from cancer may desire a return to health, but perhaps he is unwilling to undergo the very painful surgery which is indicated as necessary. In such a case he could be said to desire health, but not to truly intend it, since "when we speak of intending to have health, we mean not only that we will to have it, but that we will to have it by means of something else." [4]

It is proper to note, however, that the desire and the intention are not two separate acts, for the intention of the end and the willing of the means constitute but one single act. To will the remedy in order to have health is one single act of willing. The willing of the means blends with the intending of the end into one single act.[5]

St. Thomas defined intention thus: "Intendere est actus voluntatis in ordine ad rationem." [6] St. Bonaventure (1221-1274), the contemporary and good friend of St. Thomas, defined intention in a similar fashion: "Voluntas ratiocinata prout dirigitur in finem." Both of these definitions were embodied in the text of Pruemmer (1866-1931).[7]

Later authors have followed St. Thomas in this understanding of the intention. Lacroix (1652-1714) defined it: "Intentio est propositum seu voluntas efficax finis ut obtinendi per media." [8]

[3] "Voluntas respicit finem tripliciter . . . consideratur finis secundum quod est terminus alicujus quod in ipsum ordinatur; et sic intentio respicit finem. Non enim solum ex hoc intendere dicimur sanitatem, quia volumus eam; sed quia volumus ad eam per aliquid aliud pervenire."—St. Thomas Aquinas, *Summa Theologica*, Ia-IIae, q. 12, a. 1, ad 4.

[4] St. Thomas Aquinas, *loc. cit.*

[5] Gilson, *The Christian Philosophy of St. Thomas Aquinas* (New York: Random House, 1956), p. 253.

[6] St. Thomas Aquinas, *De Veritate*, Vivès ed. (*Opera Omnia*, Tom. IX, New York: Musurgia, 1949), q. XXII, a. 13.

[7] *Manuale Theologiae Moralis*, Vol. III (12. ed., edited by E. Münch, Friburgi Brisgoviae-Barcinone: Herder, 1955), n. 51.

[8] *Theologia Moralis* (2 vols., Coloniae, 1719), Lib. IV, n. 1324.

Another form of the definition in which are embodied the same ideas is that of Ferraris (1687-ca. 1763): "Intentio est actus voluntatis volentis aliquid facere vel fieri a se vel ab alio."[9]

Finally, the definition of Cappello brings us to the modern period and we note that, though the form varies somewhat, the concept of what constitutes an intention remains constant. He writes: "Intentio denotat voluntatis actum, quo appetitur finis per media apte ordinata."[10]

From these few examples, which are representative of the authors from the time of St. Thomas until our own decade, one finds that the idea that an intention must include not only the wishing of the object as an end, but the willing of the means for its achievement as well, is everywhere constant.

Now, an intention may be considered under several aspects. First, one may examine the intention in itself; in other words, the intention may be viewed as an act which proceeds from the will under the direction and guidance of the intellect. On the basis of such a consideration there results the threefold distinction between an actual, virtual, and habitual intention. Often included in this category by the authors is a fourth term, the interpretative intention. The interpretative intention, however, as will be shown later, as it is defined and understood by many authors who include it under this heading, is in fact no intention at all.

The intention may also be distinguished according to the end which is intended by the will. This, in other words, is a division which is derived from a consideration of the object which is represented by the intellect, and then intended by the will. Here the authors distinguish the explicit and implicit intention as well as the direct and the indirect intention.

Finally there is given a division of intention as based upon the manner in which the will is directed toward its object. Sometimes this intention is made in such a way as to be independent of any events or any circumstances; at other times it may be made in such a way as to be dependent upon them. Un-

[9] *Bibliotheca Canonica, Iuridica, Moralis, Theologica, necnon Ascetica, Polemica, Rubricistica, Historica* (9 vols., Romae, 1885-1899), s.v. *intentio*, n. 1 (hereafter cited as *Bibliotheca*).

[10] *De Sacramentis*, I, n. 38.

der this heading, then, the authors consider the absolute and the conditional intention.

B. Intention as an Act of the Will Considered in Itself

1. Actual Intention

Though St. Thomas did not set out to offer a definition of an actual intention, it is evident that he understood such an intention to include an act of the will on the part of the minister or the recipient of the sacrament as well as the attention which they give to the things which are being said or done.[11]

The definition of an actual intention given by Suarez (1548-1617) stressed the fact that the act of the will to confect the sacrament is elicited simultaneously with the performance of the external sacramental rite. "Actualis intentio consistit in hoc quod actu eliciatur voluntas faciendi sacramentum eo tempore quo exterius fit." [12]

De Lugo (1583-1660) illustrated his understanding of an actual intention with the example of the minister who has an intention to baptize at the time when he is pronouncing the words of the form and pouring the baptismal water. "Intentio actualis est qua ego actu intendo baptizare, quando profero verba et effundo aquam." [13]

Modern authors are in complete agreement in accepting the concept of an actual intention as given by the older authors. Noldin (1838-1922) for one, suggested this definition: "Actualis intentio ea dicitur quae hic et nunc exsistit, in opus influit et advertitur, quando opus peragitur." [14] Similar definitions are found among other recent writers.[15]

[11] *Summa Theologica,* III, q. 64, a. 8, ad 3.

[12] *Commentarius et Disputationes in Tertiam Partem D. Thomae* (Vivès ed., *Opera Omnia,* Tom. XX, Parisiis, 1860), Q. 64, a. 10, disp. xiii, sect. 3, n. 3 (hereafter cited as *Commentarius*).

[13] *Disputationes Scholasticae et Morales* (8 vols., Parisiis, 1868-69), *Tractatus de Sacramentis in Genere,* Disp. viii, sect. 5, n. 72 (hereafter cited as *De Sacramentis in Genere*).

[14] *Summa Theologiae Moralis* (27. ed., 3 vols., Oeniponte-Lipsiae: Rauch, 1940), III, n. 20 a.

[15] For the sake of comparison some examples of modern definitions may be given. "Intentio actualis est quae existit hic et nunc, dum ponitur

Some authors continue to subdivide the actual intention, further distinguishing the "reflex actual intention" from the "simply direct actual intention." Thus, when the recipient of baptism simply adverts to the intention which he has while being baptized, he has the simply direct actual intention.[16] When the person, in addition to adverting to his act of the will, also by reflex action now expressly and consciously wills: "I want to be baptized now" as the act is being placed, he has the reflex actual intention.[17]

From this study, then, of the definition of an actual intention as given by the authors from the period immediately after the Council of Trent (1545-1563) until the present time, certain requirements which are judged to be essential by all writers for the actual intention may be ascertained. First, the intention must be efficacious. In the case of the minister of the sacrament, the intention must be capable of allowing him to act as a true efficient cause in the administration of the sacrament. In regard to the recipient, it needs only to dispose him to freely accept and receive this boon of God's grace. Secondly, the very intention itself, and not some effect of it, must be present simultaneously with the actual performance of the intended act. Finally, the minister or the recipient of the sacrament must have an awareness of and an advertence to the presence of the intention as the sacramental act is being performed.

It may be helpful to remind the reader that some of the authors have preferred to employ a somewhat different terminology

---

actus, et quidem clare advertitur."—Cappello, *De Sacramentis,* I, n. 39; "Intentio actualis est quae hic et nunc elicitur, dum ponitur actus, et quidem clare advertitur."—Vermeersch, *Theologia Moralis* (4. ed., 4 vols., Romae: Pontificia Università Gregoriana, 1948), III, n. 166; "Quod hic et nunc procedit a voluntate cum attentione intellectus."—Genicot-Salsmans, *Institutiones Theologiae Moralis* (14. ed., 2 vols., Buenos Aires: Desclée, 1943), I, n. 10; "Est ea quae elicitur dum ritus sacramentalis peragitur."—Connell, *De Sacramentis Ecclesiae* (New York: Pustet, 1923), n. 51; "Actus voluntatis quo agens, advertens ad ea quae agit, volens agit."—Coronata, *De Sacramentis* (2. ed., 3 vols., Taurini: Marietti, 1948-51), I, n. 53.

[16] "Simpliciter actualis seu in actu exercito quae tunc habetur cum quis sciens et volens et advertens opus ponit."—Coronata, *De Sacramentis,* I, n. 53; Connell, *De Sacramentis Ecclesiae,* n. 51.

[17] Pruemmer, *Manuale Theologiae Moralis,* III, n. 63 (1).

and have chosen to call this intention defined above a formal intention. Lacroix, for one, did this because he believed the term *actual intention* was broader and should be more correctly applied so as to include both the actual intention and the virtual intention. Yet, from the definition which he offered of the formal intention, it is readily apparent that he understood the formal intention in a sense that coincides with that of an actual intention.

> Intentio formalis est voluntas efficax quae nunc in se existit et satis percipitur ab eo qui eam habet.[18]

Tournely (1658-1729), too, accepted both terms and then proceeded to define the actual or formal intention in accord with the common teaching as "praesens et actualis animi applicatio ad quod agitur." [19]

2. Virtual Intention

St. Thomas urged that, whenever it is possible, the minister of the sacraments should endeavor to possess an actual intention when he confers the sacraments. Admitting the practical difficulty in realizing this suggestion, however, he acknowledged that it suffices for the minister to have only a habitual intention. "Habet habitualem intentionem, quae sufficit ad perfectionem sacramenti." [20]

Since we know that modern authors commonly insist that the minister of the sacraments must possess at least a virtual intention for the confection of the sacraments, this statement of the Angelic Doctor may surprise us. However, the difficulty which this form of expression may cause is quickly dispelled when St. Thomas exemplifies what he means and understands by such an habitual intention.

> When a priest goes to baptize someone, he intends to do for him what the Church does. Wherefore, if subsequently during the exercise of the act his mind be distracted to

[18] Lacroix, *Theologia Moralis,* Lib. IV, n. 1324.

[19] *Praelectiones Theologicae de Sacramentis in Genere* (Parisiis, 1726), Q. 7, a. 1, Concl. secunda (hereafter cited as *Praelectiones*).

[20] *Summa Theologica,* III, q. 64, a. 8, ad 3.

> other matters, the sacrament is valid in virtue of his original intention.[21]

It is apparent from this example that St. Thomas was speaking of what the authors of subsequent periods have come to call a virtual intention. "In exemplo ab Angelico Doctore allato manifeste habetur intentio virtualis et non habitualis in sensu modernorum." [22]

Despite the efforts of several commentators on St. Thomas, notably Billuart (1685-1757),[23] to explain the presence of this term by ascribing it to the error of a later scribe, it seems certain that in the 13th century the term *intentio habitualis* was so employed as to include both the virtual intention and the habitual intention of the modern writers.[24]

Many of the earlier definitions given for the virtual intention offer only a partial expression of the requirements for such an intention. That, however, given by Cardinal de Lugo clearly states three essential requirements for the virtual intention. According to the definition of de Lugo, the virtual intention is one which has actually been elicited in the past. Next, it is one which has never been revoked by means of a contrary intention or in any other way. Finally, it endures and continues to exist in such a way as to influence the work which was the original object of the actual intention, and which now is taking place.

> Intentio virtualis est intentio quae non solum est praeterita non retractata, sed manet in virtute et influens in opus quod nunc fit.[25]

In the somewhat lengthy definition given by Laymann (1574-

[21] *Loc. cit.*

[22] Pruemmer, *Manuale Theologiae Moralis,* III, n. 63 (2).

[23] *Summa Sancti Thomae* (Parisiis, n.d.), *Tractatus de Sacramentis in Communi,* Diss. v, art. 7, par. 3 (hereafter cited as *De Sacramentis in Communi*).

[24] "S. Thomas cum antiquis theologis non raro promiscue sumunt intentionem habitualem et virtualem."—Cappello, *De Sacramentis,* I, p. 36, note 5. According to Coronata it was Scotus (1266-1308) who introduced the term *virtual intention.—De Sacramentis,* I, p. 35, note 3.

[25] De Lugo, *De Sacramentis in Genere,* Disp. viii, n. 73.

1635), one may find two new and most important ideas. First of all, Laymann in his definition stressed what is in fact the essential distinction between the actual and the virtual intention, namely, that in the virtual intention there is lacking in the minister or in the recipient of the sacrament the advertence to or the awareness of the intention which is the cause of the action or the disposition which is required. Furthermore, he indicated the criterion which later was to be found more fully stated in other authors, namely the criterion by which one can determine whether the act has taken place with a virtual intention or only a habitual intention. He stated that a virtual intention is present when the person is in such a state of mind that, with distractions duly overcome, he can become aware again of the original intention by virtue of which he is performing these sacramental acts.

> Intentio virtualis ea est in qua minister nunc quidem non attendit, agit tamen ex antecedente rationali attentione ac proposito; atque in ea dispositione est ut iam quoque attendere posset, nisi animus ad alia distractus.[26]

Again the definitions given by modern authors are very similar to those cited above. One may again take that of Noldin as an example: "Virtualis ea dicitur, quae hic et nunc exsistit, in opus influit, at non advertitur quando opus ponitur." [27]

[26] Laymann, *Theologia Moralis* (6. ed., Bambergae, 1669), Lib. V, *De Sacramentis et Sacrificio Novae Legis*, tr. I, c. 5, n. 11 (hereafter cited as *Theologia Moralis*).

[27] *Summa Theologiae Moralis,* III, n. 20 b. For the sake of further comparison one may again cite the definitions given by other recent authors. "Si existit hic et nunc ac revera in opus influit, at non advertitur dum opus ponitur."—Cappello, *De Sacramentis,* I, n. 39; "Ea dicitur quae nunc revera in opus influit, sed non advertitur, dum opus ponitur."—Vermeersch, *Theologia Moralis,* III, n. 166; "Illud quod procedit a volitione ad quam iam non attenditur, sed quae in effectu aliquo suo, hic et nunc posito a volente, perseverat."—Genicot-Salsmans, *Institutiones Theologiae Moralis,* I, n. 10; " . . quae procedit ex intentione actuali praevie elicita cujus virtus seu vis in actionem sacramentum administrandi influit."—Connell, *De Sacramentis Ecclesiae,* n. 51; "Quae aut reflexe aut direct actualiter habita initio operis quod intenditur, non fuit quidem retractata, at non fuit de novo elicita, sed potius non amplius fuit ab agente percepta; de facto tamen in agente ad opus perficiendum influit."—Coronata, *De Sacramentis,* I, n. 53.

An analysis of the definitions of the modern authors as well as of their predecessors reveals that four elements are demanded for any satisfactory understanding of the concept of a virtual intention. It is first of all necessary that an actual intention has been elicited at some earlier time. Furthermore, there must never later have been elicited any contrary intention which would have revoked this prior intention. Moreover, there must be no advertence or awareness of the intention whose power still influences the act. Finally, it is required that some sort of energy or force remain from the original actual intention and now exercise some truly causal influence in the performance of the sacramental act.

The difference again between the actual and the virtual intention lies in this, that an actual intention includes two elements, the act of the will as well as attention or the reflex consideration of the act which is being performed; the virtual intention includes only the act of the will, but no attention.

> Discrimen patet inter utramque: Actuale duo importat, scil., voluntatem et attentionem seu reflexam considerationem actionis quae agitur; virtualis importat solum voluntatem, non vero attentionem ad hanc ipsam voluntatem et actionem ab ea procedentem.[28]

Though in the defining of the virtual intention one can find complete agreement among the authors, no such unanimity is apparent when they come to discuss the further question as to how the original actual intention continues to be present in a virtual intention, and how, though not adverted to by the minister, it still continues to direct the human faculties in the performance of the sacramental rites in a truly human manner.

According to Suarez the individual by his actual intention sets into motion his external powers in order to achieve a certain desired goal. In the course of his activity, however, he may no longer continue to advert to that goal, but nevertheless his efforts to attain it are continued in the acts of these external powers. His external activity now is no longer dependent upon any actual intention or internal act of the will. His original actual intention is now to be found in his external powers, which are con-

[28] Cappello, *De Sacramentis,* I, n. 39.

tinuing their activity to achieve the goal which was the object of his original intention.[29]

The person applies his external powers to the performance of an act through his intention. These same powers continue to operate and tend to bring about the completion of that act until the original intention is either revoked or interrupted, as, for example, when the minister is distracted while baptizing. But as long as these external powers continue to operate under the influence of the previous intention, so long can it be said that the act is being performed with a virtual intention.[30]

The original intention elicited by an act of the will retains its efficacy until such a time as either the act itself is completed and the desired goal is attained, or a contrary intention is elicited, or, finally, there arises an impeding factor which interrupts the act. At such a time then a new intention will be required if the act is to be continued or begun again.[31] According to Sporer (ca. 1620-1683), Vazquez (1551-1605) held a view which was very similar to that of Suarez. He also taught that by virtue of the original actual intention the external powers were directed toward the particular act, and that, even after the individual was no longer aware of this earlier intention, still the faculties continued to be applied to the performance of the act as a result of that intention.[32]

De Coninck (1571-1633) believed that in those acts which were performed with only a virtual intention there was to be found a certain connection between the original actual intention and the actions which followed, a certain linking together, as it were, of all the intermediate acts which were performed between the time of the eliciting of the first intention and that of the completion of the act which had been first intended.[33] Though Sporer

[29] Suarez, *Commentarius,* Q. 64, a. 10, disp. xiii, sect. 3, n. 6.

[30] Suarez, *loc. cit.*

[31] Suarez, *loc. cit.*

[32] Sporer, *Theologia Moralis Sacramentalis* (3. ed., Salisburgi, 1711), Pars I, c. 2, sect. 3, n. 107.

[33] "Aliqui putant esse connexionem quandam inter primam intentionem actualem et actiones subsequentes, seu concatenationem quandam actionum intermediarum inter primam intentionem et ultimum opus intentum."—Sporer, *Theologia Moralis Sacramentalis,* Pars I, c. 2, sect. 3, n. 107.

openly confessed that he failed to understand the opinion of De Coninck,[34] De Lugo believed that De Coninck found the original actual intention to continue present at least in the imagination.[35] The former intention, then, is said to be virtually present by reason of the impress upon the imagination which remains behind from the first proposal to perform the act. It is this residual element still abiding in the imagination which brings it about that the person performs all those acts which he in the beginning proposed to perform by his actual intention.

According to this view the human will has originally set the imagination in motion, and by reason of this original application the imagination now directs the whole series of acts which follow. Thus, it can be said that the entire series of acts proceeds from the first intention in a truly human fashion. Despite the distractions which may occur, as a result of which there is little or no advertence to the intention, nevertheless the imagination by its acquired habits directs external acts in order to achieve the proposed goal.[36]

Dicastillus (1585-1653) preferred to explain this residual element as rather the original actual intention. It is now, however, so weak and feeble, as it were, that the human agent no longer adverts to its presence. Nonetheless, despite his lack of awareness of its presence, it is still capable of an active influence upon the acts which the person has intended earlier to perform. Dicastillus wrote:

> Probabilissimum mihi videtur intentionem virtualem . . . nihil aliud esse quam voluntatem quidem actualem remissam tamen et cum remissa advertentia faciendi illa quae ex habitu iam cognoscuntur esse necessaria ad statutum finem.[37]

Sporer mentioned Gobat (1600-1679) as also holding this opinion, for he wrote:

> Dicastillus et Gobat expresse docent intentionem quamcumque virtualem esse ipsam intentionem actualem, sed ita

[34] *Loc. cit.*

[35] De Lugo, *De Sacramentis in Genere,* Disp. viii, n. 87.

[36] De Lugo, *De Sacramentis in Genere,* Disp. viii, n. 87.

[37] Cited by Gobat, *Opera Moralia* (2 vols., Venetiis, 1749), Tom. I, Tr. 1, *de sacramentis in genere,* sect. 3, n. 65.

> remissam ac tenuem et debilem ut non advertatur amplius adesse et tamen revera, modo tamen vix perceptibili, nunc moveat et influat in opus intentum.[38]

An examination, however, of the text of Gobat reveals that he simply quoted the words of Dicastillus, as given above, and then mentioned the view held by other writers, but did not express any preference in regard to either opinion.[39] Among modern writers this view has been adopted by Lehmkuhl (1834-1918).[40]

According to a number of authors this was also the view which was held by De Lugo. Thus Sporer wrote:

> (De Lugo) arbitratur entitatem esse actus intellectus et voluntatis tenuissimos, remanentes ex prima intentione circa tale opus intentum.[41]

It is true that De Lugo acknowledged that the virtual intention may in fact be at times simply an actual intention in which the act of the will is so weak and tenuous as to be no longer adverted to by the person who elicited the intention.

> Hoc enim sufficiet ad declarandum quomodo intentio et voluntas praeterita maneat virtualiter et influat in actionem praesentem: nam vel manet in aliquo actu voluntatis praesenti tenuissimo et confuso. . . .[42]

In this very same context, however, he also acknowledged that the actual intention may continue to be present only in the imagination and in the material appetites.

> Si vero dicatur non perseverare ullum actum voluntatis praesentem, quando actio sacramentalis continuatur, sed solum actum imaginativae et appetitus materialis, in his ipsis actibus manet virtualiter voluntas prior.[43]

[38] *Theologia Moralis Sacramentalis,* Pars I, c. 2, sect. 3, n. 107.

[39] Gobat, *loc. cit.*

[40] *Theologia Moralis,* Vol. II (9. ed., Friburgi-Brisgoviae, 1898), n. 48.

[41] *Theologia Moralis Sacramentalis,* Pars I, c. 2, sect. 3, n. 107; cf. also Lanza, *Theologia Moralis,* I (Taurini-Romae: Marietti, 1949), n. 55; Vermeersch, *Theologia Moralis,* I, n. 44.

[42] De Lugo, *De Sacramentis in Genere,* Disp. viii, n. 87.

[43] *De Sacramentis in Genere,* Disp. viii, n. 87.

In his conclusion De Lugo indicated that he believed the original intention may be said to continue in a virtual manner in two ways, either as a very weak remainder of the original intention which is no longer adverted to, or as an act of the will which is found in the material appetite and which bids the continued performance of the acts demanded to achieve the aim intended in the prior act of the will.

> . . . id tamen sufficit ut homo dicatur continuare actionem illam ex intentione et voluntate praeterita, quae ideo dicitur virtualiter manere, quia adest praesens aliqua virtus ab ea relicta, scilicet, vel actus voluntatis confusus, vel actus voluntatis in appetitu imperans prosecutionem actionis cum ordine et respectu ad priorem intentionem.[44]

Tournely in his view seemed to be influenced in part by the teaching of Suarez, in part by the teaching of De Lugo, for he wrote:

> Dicendum est voluntatem praeteritam perseverare quidem remote in potentiis externis quae continuant motus suos, sed etiam proxime in actu voluntatis praesenti, tenuissimo et confuso, quo volumus voluntate actuali inchoatum opus perficere.[45]

Finally, Vermeersch (1858-1936) indicated that he believed the solution was to be found in the fact that, by the association of ideas and images, when we bid the performance of one principal act, at the same time we determine an entire series of partial actions.[46]

3. Habitual Intention

The definition given by De Lugo of the habitual intention, though brief, is quite adequate—"intentio mere praeterita et non revocata." [47] At first glance this definition could seem to be insufficient, for it does not appear to indicate clearly the distinction

[44] *Loc. cit.*

[45] Tournely, *Praelectiones,* Q. vii, art. 1, concl. prima.

[46] "Consociatio idearum et imaginum nobis facilitatem affert, ut uno imperandi actu omnem seriem actionem partialium, quae satis saepe fecerimus, determinare possimus."—Vermeersch, *Theologia Moralis,* I, n. 44.

[47] De Lugo, *De Sacramentis in Genere,* Disp. viii, n. 72.

between this intention and the previously discussed virtual intention. This latter intention is also an intention which has been elicited in the past and never revoked. However, De Lugo in his definition by the use of the adverb *mere* demonstrates that a habitual intention is one which is to be regarded as operative solely in the past, since it has no present direct influence or efficacy.

The definition given by Suarez is much longer and more explicit in pointing out the differences between the habitual and the virtual intention. Thus it aids our understanding of both forms of intention. According to Suarez, a habitual intention exists when an actual intention has preceded, and in this regard the habitual intention is identified with the virtual intention. However, unlike the virtual intention, the habitual intention has no influence in any way on the external action which may now take place. There is no force, no energy, no *virtus,* remaining from the earlier actual intention, either in the memory or in the intellect and will.

> Habitualis intentio dicitur esse quando praecessit voluntas faciendi sacramentum et postea nullo modo influit in effectum, seu in actionem externam quia neque ullo modo est postea in memoria, seu cogitatione hominis, nec per se aut per aliquem effectum seu virtutem relictam, est causa talis actionis.[48]

The habitual intention, therefore, as Noldin pointed out, is not here and now in existence, and hence cannot have any influence on the act. "Habitualis illa dicitur quae aliquando habita et numquam retractata est, sed hic et nunc non exsistit et proinde in opus non influit."[49] Similar definitions can be found among all modern authors.[50]

[48] Suarez, *Commentarius,* Q. 64, a. 10, disp. xiii, sect. 3, n. 3.

[49] Noldin-Schmitt, *Summa Theologiae Moralis,* III, n. 20 c.

[50] "Quae olim habita est et numquam fuit retractata atque adhuc perdurat, at hic et nunc nec advertitur nec influit positive in actum humanum qua talem."—Cappello, *De Sacramentis,* I, n. 39; "Quae aliquando quidem habita et numquam retractata fuit, sed iam nullo modo in opus positive influit."—Pruemmer, *Manuale Theologiae Moralis,* III, n. 63 (3); "Quae antea elicita numquam retractata est sed hic et nunc in opus nullatenus influit."—Vermeersch, *Theologia Moralis,* III, n. 166; "Ea quae prius elicita

The definitions given by the several authors, then, demonstrate the requirements for a habitual intention. First of all, it is required that an actual intention has previously been elicited. Secondly, this prior intention must never have been revoked. Finally, this intention which was elicited earlier must not now have any influence upon the act. It must not have any positive effect upon this human action.

It is possible, however, that the prior intention which is now only a habitual intention could affect a human action in so far as it would serve as a predisposition for such an act. Furthermore, it is important to note the expression "human action," since the prior intention might have some influence on an action performed later when the person who elicited the intention becomes drunk or insane or otherwise incapable of a truly human act.[51]

As has been pointed out earlier, it is in regard to this third requirement, viz., that the prior intention must not influence the performing of a sacramental act, that there is to be found the basic distinction between the virtual intention and the habitual intention.

4. Interpretative Intention

A number of quite variant definitions of the interpretative intention can be found among the works of the different authors. This variety arises from the fact that the different authors are applying the same term to entirely different types of intention; it does not arise from any disagreement concerning its nature. Many authors understand the interpretative intention as an intention presumed *de futuro;* others, as an intention presumed *de praesenti;* still others, and this would include the two great

---

fuit et non retractata est: nihilominus in confectionem ritus sacramentalis fluit."—Connell, *De Sacramentis Ecclesiae,* n. 51; "Quae aliquando posita fuit nec retractata, sed iam nullo modo in opus influit aut influere potest."—Coronata, *De Sacramentis,* I, n. 53.

[51] It may be of help to recall the meaning of an *actus humanus.* "Dicuntur actus humani qui saltem quoad modum hominis sunt proprii, i.e. qui a libera voluntate procedunt."—Lanza, *Theologia Moralis,* I, n. 53.

names of De Lugo[52] and Suarez,[53] use the term in the meaning of an indirect intention, or what more recent authors would term a *voluntarium indirectum* or a *voluntarium in causa.*[54]

Consideration will first be given to those authors who understand the interpretative intention in the sense of a presumed intention *de futuro.* Noldin defined it in such a sense.

> Intentio interpretativa ea dicitur quae numquam adfuit, quae tamen propter quandam inclinationem voluntatis in objectum adesset, si illud in mentem veniret.[55]

From this definition it appears that in the mind of the author the so-called interpretative intention is actually and in fact no intention at all. Rather, it is on the part of the person only a predisposition of his will to have an intention.[56] On the part of others, it is a judgment based upon the apparent disposition of this person, that he would elicit such an intention, if only he would advert to the need or usefulness of it. It is a judgment that, though an intention is not actually present, yet, because of the apparent disposition of the person such an intention would be present, provided only the proper situation would present itself.

A similar understanding of the interpretative intention is held by many modern authors. Coronata, for example, gives this definition: "Quae numquam actualiter habita fuit; haberet tamen quis eam si de ea cogitare posset, et proinde praesumitur eam habere." [57]

Other authors, however, including St. Alphonsus (1696-1787), defined this intention in almost identical terms, only later to use the expression in a different sense. St. Alphonsus wrote: "Intentio interpretativa habetur cum quis nullam habet nec habuit intentionem actualem, sed ita est dispositus ut si adver-

[52] *De Sracramentis in Genere,* Disp. viii, n. 73.

[53] *Commentarius,* Q. 64, a. 10, disp. xiii, sect. 3, n. 2.

[54] Cappello, *De Sacramentis,* I, n. 36, note 8.

[55] *Summa Theologiae Moralis,* III, n. 20 d.

[56] "Voluntatis dispositio ad eam intentionem habendam."—Cappello, *De Sacramentis,* I, n. 36.

[57] Coronata, *De Sacramentis,* I, n. 53.

teret, haberet."[58] Others, too, e.g., Lacroix[59] and Pruemmer,[60] defined the interpretative intention in the same way. However, though all agreed that an intention is required for the reception of any and all of the sacraments, and despite their own definitions of the interpretative intention, St. Alphonsus stated that an interpretative intention sufficed for the reception of confirmation and extreme unction conferred on the dying,[61] Lacroix acknowledged its sufficiency for the reception of the Eucharist by the dying,[62] and Pruemmer regarded it as sufficing for the reception of any and all of the sacraments.[63]

Actually, these authors were making use of the term "interpretative intention" in a second sense, which is explained by Connell:

> In altero sensu, intentio interpretativa est ea quae numquam explicite elicita fuit, sed tamen rationabiliter praesumitur adesse implicite in aliqua intentione generali quam persona (habitualiter saltem) revera habet. Sic intellecta, intentio interpretativa aequivalet intentioni habituali implicitae. . . .[64]

Merkelbach (1871-1942) was another who indicated that the solution lies in the realization that authors were using the same term in two totally different meanings, and that those authors

[58] *Theologia Moralis* (ed. L. Gaudé, 4 vols., Romae, 1905-1912), Lib. VI, n. 15.

[59] *Theologia Moralis,* Lib. IV, n. 1324: "Interpretativa intentio est quam homo numquam habuit, est tamen ita comparatus animo ut eam haberet si de ea cogitaret."

[60] "Interpretativa vocatur illa intentio, quae nec est nunc nec antea fuit, quae tamen, ut praesumitur ex claris indiciis, adesset, si homo hic et nunc attenderet aut attendere posset."—*Manuale Theologiae Moralis,* III, n. 63 (4).

[61] *Theologia Moralis,* Lib. VI, n. 82.

[62] "Ad Eucharistiam requiritur saltem habitualis intentio. Attamen in moribundo etiam interpretativam sufficere . . ."—*Theologia Moralis,* Lib. VI, n. 170.

[63] "Ad sacramenta suscipienda (saltem in casu necessitatis) sufficit quaelibet ex istis quattuor intentionibus;"—*Manuale Theologiae Moralis,* III, n. 63 (4).

[64] *De Sacramentis Ecclesiae,* n. 51.

who held for the sufficiency of the interpretative intention for the reception of some of the sacraments were actually speaking of what authors called the habitual implicit intention.

> Quod si aliquando dicant quodammodo sufficere interpretativam, est lis de verbis: ita loquuntur improprie, et non intelligunt mere interpretativam de futuro, sed praesumptam de praesenti, qua aliquis, secundum habitualem notitiam et dispositionem praesentem christiane vivendi, explicite peteret sacramentum si ab ipso quaereretur;—sed ista est habitualis implicita, quae ob conjecturalia signa praesentia adesse praesumitur.[65]

The implicit habitual intention is presumed to be present, to be actually had and possessed right now, on account of some preceding fact or because of the dispositions of the person. The interpretative intention is one that presumably would be had in the future, though it is not had right now. It would be elicited if the object were proposed or if the person would think sufficiently on the matter.[66]

In the sense, therefore, of a true interpretative intention, it seems that the authors require two essential elements to be embodied in the concept. First, it is postulated that there was no eliciting of any previous actual intention. Secondly, it is postulated, on the basis of the individual's known dispositions, that one could justly conclude that such an intention would be elicited, if he were to think about it.

C. Intention According to the Object Willed or Intended

1. *Explicit and Implicit Intention*

The object of the intention may be something which is clearly seen, known and understood. On the other hand, that which is

[65] *Summa Theologiae Moralis* (8. ed., 3 vols., Montréal: Desclée, 1949), I, n. 93.

[66] "Habituale implicitum dicitur etiam et recte, praesumptum de praesenti, eo quod nunc coniicitur adesse ex praecedente aliquo facto vel dispositione subjecti; interpretativum vero idem est ac praesumptum de futuro eo quod coniicitur futurum fuisse, etsi reapse nullum fuit, si objectum propositum esset, vel, ut diximus, de eo sufficienter quis cogitasset vel cogitare posset. Utrumque autem dicitur praesumptum, quia praesumitur suo modo adesse."—Iorio, *Theologia Moralis* (4. ed., 3 vols., Neapoli: D'Auria, 1953-54), I, n. 18.

intended may at times be known and understood at best in a rather vague and confused manner. In such a case it may be intended not so much in itself, but, since it is so vaguely known, it may be intended only in so far as it is contained in some other object which is better known. When the object intended is something clearly known and understood, then the intention is called an explicit or express intention.

> Expressa intentio est qua rem aliquam cogitatam et cognitam vis et intendis, non in alio, sed in seipso, quia scilicet illam cognoscis, de illa cogitas, et illam cognoscens facis necessaria ad eam efficiendam, acquirendam.[67]

When the object intended is known only in a confused manner, then the intention is called implicit, and this Gobat defines:

> Implicita intentio est illa qua aliquid intendis, elicis, proponis, cupis, aut vis, non expresse cogitans de illo, sed de alio in quo est volitum seu cum quo est vel naturaliter vel per humanam legem connexum.[68]

Thus, when the young man approaches the bishop at the altar to receive the subdiaconate, his intention is to receive the order. This is an object of his intention which he clearly understands and fully comprehends. In short, he explicitly intends to receive this order. At the same time, however, he may have only a confused knowledge of some of the obligations which are intimately connected with this particular order, especially the most grave obligations of celibacy and of the recitation of the Divine Office. Inasmuch as these obligations are intimately bound up with the order by the positive law of the Church, he, simultaneously with his explicit intention to receive the subdiaconate, has an implicit intention to accept these additional burdens as well.

The object, then, which is implicitly intended may be one which is bound up with the object explicitly intended either as a result of positive human ordinance or by the law of nature.[69]

[67] Gobat, *Opera Moralia,* Tom. I, Tr. 1, *de sacramentis in genere,* sect. 3, n. 66. It should be here noted that Gobat (1600-1679) used the term *expressa,* whereas other authors preferred *explicita.* A shorter definition is that given by Lacroix: "Intentio explicita est qua aliquid in se clare cognitum volumus."—*Theologia Moralis,* Lib. IV, n. 1324.

[68] *Opera Moralia,* Tom. I, Tr. 1, *de sacramentis in genere,* sect. 3, n. 66.

[69] Gobat, *loc. cit.*

The cited example of the subdiaconate and its concomitant obligations is an example wherein positive human law has bound and joined the objects of the intention together. Marriage is an excellent example wherein the same result has been achieved by the law of nature. The parties, if they have the explicit intention to marry, have also the implicit intention to accept the rights and duties which belong by the very law of nature to the married state, e.g., the obligation of the procreation and education of offspring.

2. Direct and Indirect Intention

De Lugo considered the case wherein a priest would know that every time upon getting drunk he would recite the words of consecration. If, then, the priest intended to drink enough to become drunk, one could ask whether at least an indirect intention to consecrate the Eucharist was contained in the direct intention to get drunk. Such an intention was called by some an indirect intention, by others an interpretative intention, and by others a *voluntarium in causa.*

According to De Lugo a person has an indirect intention when he wills a cause which he foresees will produce certain effects: "Intentio indirecta vel interpretativa ea dicitur quando aliquis vult causam ex qua praevidet sequi talem effectum."[70] The object which the person wills and which is at the same time the cause of the foreseen later effect is thus directly willed or intended, and thus is known as the direct intention.

> Directa intentio est qua aliquid volumus directe, formaliter, positive et explicite.[71]

The distinction between the implicit intention and the indirect intention consists in this that, whereas in the implicit intention the person wills an object which contains in itself other objects concerning which the individual has at the most a confused knowledge, and to which he has not given an express thought, in the indirect intention he wills and intends the prin-

[70] De Lugo, *De Sacramentis in Genere,* Disp. viii, n. 100.

[71] Gobat, *Opera Moralia,* Tom. I, Tr. 1, *de sacramentis in genere,* sect. 3, n. 67.

cipal or direct object from which he clearly foresees that there will follow and flow a certain number of consequences as so many effects of his action.[72] On the other hand, the direct intention is to be considered identical with the explicit or express intention.[73]

D. Intention According to the Manner in Which it is Elicited

The intention can at times be made in such a way as to be independent of any facts, events, or circumstances. This intention is called an absolute intention. This, of course, is the usual form in which an intention is made. There may, however, be doubts as to the fact of a previous baptism, or regarding the presence of a sufficient intention, or even whether the person is still living. In order to prevent irreverence to the sacrament, the minister then confers it with the use of an appended condition. This condition suspends the efficacy of the sacramental act unless a certain fact, element, quality, or the like, which is the basis of the condition, is verified. In the conditional intention the act is made dependent upon the fulfillment or the verification of the condition which has been joined to the intention.

> Intentio conditionata est illa sola quae habet adjunctam conditionem proprie dictam seu quae non est efficax, nisi existat conditio sub qua seu dependenter a qua elicitur.[74]

Sometimes the condition will be expressed in such a way as to suspend the efficacy of the sacramental act until actual knowledge of its verification is acquired and sometimes only the verification of the condition is required. This becomes clearer from the definition given by Sporer (ca. 1620-1683).

> Conditionata intentio est ea qua volumus et intendimus aliquid solum dependenter a tali vel tali conditione, ita ut nostrum velle non sit efficax, nisi illa conditio ponatur, vel posita esse cognoscatur.[75]

[72] Sporer, *Theologia Moralis Sacramentalis,* Pars I, c. 2, sect. 3, n. 111.

[73] Sporer, *loc. cit.*

[74] Sporer, *Theologia Moralis Sacramentalis,* Pars I, c. 2, sect. 3, n. 111.

[75] *Theologia Moralis Sacramentalis,* Pars I, c. 2, sect. 3, n. 112.

The absolute intention, however, is made without any such added suspensive element, and thus, in regard to its efficacy, is independent of all conditions.

> Voluntas fertur in objectum pure ac simpliciter, independenter, scil., a quolibet eventu aut circumstantia.[76]

[76] Cappello, *De Sacramentis,* I, n. 37.

CHAPTER II

THE REQUISITES OF INTENTION FOR INFANTS AND THE PERPETUALLY INSANE

A. Infants Cannot Elicit a True Intention

"Before the completion of his seventh year of age a person is called an infant (*infans, puer, parvulus*) and is presumed not to enjoy the use of reason."[1] Obviously, then, it is not possible to speak of the necessity for infants to have a personal intention to receive the sacraments. Since they lack the use of reason, they cannot be expected to give that same consent which is required of adults for the valid reception of the sacraments. Being incapable of human acts, they are thereby incapable of eliciting a true intention.

Some theologians, confronted with the dilemma of admitting both the universal necessity of baptism for salvation on the one hand, and also the necessity of an intention for the valid reception of the sacraments on the other, have assumed the granting of a special illumination to infants when dying before they attain the use of reason. Nowhere, however, do they offer any real proof for this assertion.

Other theologians, found notably among the sects of the Anabaptists and Baptists, have denied that infants are capable of receiving any of the sacraments validly.

B. Infants are Capable of Receiving Some Sacraments Validly

1. Baptism

Tradition testifies to the early practice in the Church of conferring baptism upon infants. Origen (185-254) claimed that this custom was received from the Apostles themselves. "Ecclesia ab Apostolis traditionem suscepit etiam parvulis Baptismum

[1] Can. 88, § 3.

dare."[2] According to Leeming, "by the end of the second century, the evidence is clear that the Christian Church regarded infants as proper subjects for baptism."[3] This was the constant teaching and the unbroken practice of the Church from this early age up until the Council of Trent. Reacting against the errors of the Protestants, the Council condemned the following proposition: "If anyone says that children recently born from the wombs of their mothers are not to be baptized, let him be anathema."[4] Then it continued:

> If anyone says that children, because they have not the act of believing, are not after having received baptism to be numbered among the faithful, and that for this reason are to be re-baptized when they have reached the years of discretion; or that it is better that the baptism of such be omitted than that, while not believing by their own act, they should be baptized in the faith of the Church alone, let him be anathema.[5]

This constant teaching and unbroken practice of the Church in regard to infant baptism finds abundant expression in the Code of Canon Law. Canon 746, for example, deals with the baptism of infants in the mother's womb; canon 747, with the baptism of aborted foetuses; canon 748, with the baptism of abnormal foetuses; canon 749, with the baptism of foundlings; and canons 750 and 751, with the baptism of the infants born of heretics, schismatics, and infidels. Finally, canon 770 insists that parents must see to it that their infant children receive baptism as quickly as possible, and all authors recognize that in this precept a serious obligation is contained. There can be

[2] *In Romanos comment.*, Lib. 5, n. 9, in Lennerz, *De Sacramento Baptismi* (2. ed., Romae, 1948), p. 80.

[3] *Principles of Sacramental Theology* (Westminster, Md.: Newman, 1956), p. 64.

[4] Conc. Trident., sess. VII, *de baptismo*, can. 13—Mansi, *Sacrorum Conciliorum Nova et Amplissima Collectio* (53 vols. in 59, Parisiis, Arnhemii, Lipsiae, 1901-1927), XXXIII, 54; Schroeder, *Canons and Decrees of the Council of Trent* (St. Louis: Herder, 1941), p. 54 (hereafter cited as *Canons and Decrees*).

[5] *Loc. cit.*

no doubt that the Church's teaching concerning the validity of infant baptism is most clearly and unquestionably stated in the Code.

2. *Confirmation*

It was customary in the early Church to confer the sacrament of confirmation upon infants immediately after their baptism. This custom can be traced back in the Latin Church at least to the period of Tertullian (ca. 160–ca. 230). This usage was retained throughout the entire Church both in the East and in the West until the XIII century.[6] This custom has been retained, in the discipline of all the Eastern Churches, with the sole exception of the Maronites, wherein it is the practice still to confer confirmation upon infants immediately after they have received baptism.[7] This usage, however, has been on the wane in the Latin Church and has now virtually disappeared everywhere, being limited to Spain and those territories which have come under Hispanic influence. In these regions, however, the practice of infant confirmation has received express approval from the Holy See. The Congregation for the Discipline of the Sacraments was asked: "Whether the custom, very old in Spain and obtaining in other places, of administering the sacrament of confirmation to infants before the use of reason, can be followed." In line with canon 5, the Congregation replied that the practice of infant-confirmation could still be followed, with the proviso that attempts be made to bring about conformity with the general law of the Latin Church.[8]

The general law as it now obtains in the Church concerning the age for the reception of confirmation finds expression in canon 788.

[6] Cappello, *De Sacramentis,* I, n. 205, 3. In this regard Benedict XIV wrote: "Certum est olim tam adultos quam pueros statim post Baptismum fuisse confirmatos."—Benedictus XIV, *De Synodo Dioecesana* (2 vols., Romae, 1748), Lib. VII, c. 10, n. 3.

[7] Cappello, *De Sacramentis,* I, n. 784, 1.

[8] S. C. de Sacr., resp., 30 iun. 1932—*AAS,* XXIV, 271; Bouscaren, *The Canon Law Digest,* Vol. I (Milwaukee: Bruce, 1934), 349.

> Although the administration of the sacrament of confirmation should preferably be postponed in the Latin Church till about the seventh year of age, nevertheless it can be conferred before that age if the infant is in danger of death, or if its administration seems to the minister justified for good and serious reasons.

In addition to the common law, Pope Pius XII has granted the power to local ordinaries in the mission fields to grant faculties to their priests to confer the sacrament of confirmation upon both adults and infants who are in danger of death.[9]

Moreover, the Holy Father, in response to a petition of the hierarchy of the United States, granted for a limited period (one year) that in maternity hospitals for parturient women, and also in the orphanages of their dioceses, the sacrament of confirmation might validly and licitly be administered by the chaplains of those institutions to the children who are received there and who are in the circumstances mentioned in the decree *Spiritus Sancti munera* (1946).[10]

The Code, therefore, acknowledges the validity of infant confirmation. It limits, however, its licit bestowal, outside of a lawful divergent custom, to those cases wherein there is present a danger of death, or some other serious cause, as seen and recognized by the minister of the sacrament.[11]

3. Holy Orders

The capacity of infants to receive Holy Orders was already recognized by the early Church. The II Council of Toledo (527/531) had required that those who were ordained to minor orders as infants be provided with the opportunity of ratifying their ordination when they reached the age of eighteen for the acceptance of the burdens of their clerical state. There was never any question about the validity of these ordinations; the

[9] S. C. de Prop. Fide, decr., 18 dec. 1947—*AAS,* XL (1948), 41; Bouscaren, *The Canon Law Digest,* III (Milwaukee: Bruce, 1953), 314.

[10] S. C. de Sacr., 18 nov. 1948—Bouscaren, *The Canon Law Digest, Supplements* through 1955 (Milwaukee: Bruce, 1954-1956), under canon 782. Early in 1950 a one-year renewal, and early in 1951 and 1954 three-year renewals of this faculty were granted. See Bouscaren, *ibid.,* note.

[11] Wernz-Vidal, *Ius Canonicum,* Tom. IV, 1 (Romae, 1934), n. 56.

only doubt was whether the recipient likewise contracted the concomitant obligations of the state.[12]

More than a millennium later, Benedict XIV recounted the practice, as found in the Coptic Church, of conferring all the orders up to the diaconate upon certain infants immediately after their baptism. He declared that such ordinations were to be regarded as valid. In support of his contention he pointed to the common teaching of the canonists and theologians.

> Concordi theologorum et canonistarum suffragio definitum est validam sed illicitam censeri hanc Ordinationem, dummodo nullo laboret substantiali defectu materiae, formae et intentionis in Episcopo ordinante.[13]

He noted that additional support for the view which favored the validity could be found in the fact that this was the doctrine sanctioned by the practice of the Tribunals and Congregations of the Roman Curia. "Non attenta contraria sententia . . . quae supremis Tribunalibus et Congregationibus Urbis numquam arrisit." [14]

There seems to be no convincing reason for denying the capacity of infants to receive Orders.[15] Hence Coronata holds that the capacity of infants to receive Orders is to be regarded as a certain conclusion: ". . . ut certum affirmandum est infantes valide quamvis illicite ordinari posse." [16]

Despite the constant practice of the Church and the unanimity of the authors in acknowledging the validity of infants' ordinations in general, some hesitancy remains in regard to the capacity of infants for the reception of the Order of the episcopate This doubt arises from the fact that St. Thomas denied the validity of such an ordination. He reasoned thus:

[12] Canon 1 of this Council—Mansi, *Sacrorum Conciliorum Nova et Amplissima Collectio,* VIII, 785.

[13] *Benedicti XIV Pont. Opt. Max. Bullarium,* Tom. I, *in quo continentur Constitutiones, Epistolae, etc. editae ab initio Pontificatus usque ad annum 1746* (Prati, 1845), p. 520.

[14] *Loc. cit.*

[15] Cappello, *De Sacramentis,* IV (2. ed., Romae: Marietti, 1947), n. 357.

[16] *De Sacramentis,* II (2. ed., Taurini: Marietti, 1949), n. 57 b.

> For the episcopate, in which there is also received a power over the Mystical Body, there is required also an act on the part of the one who receives the pastoral care; and, therefore, it is also necessary for the episcopal consecration that its recipient have the use of reason.[17]

In answer to this difficulty, Cappello points out that it is not the actual pastoral care, but only the pastoral power which is conferred in the episcopal consecration, and for this no true consent or intention is strictly required. The later Thomistic writers and other distinguished commentators have interpreted the Angelic Doctor in the same fashion as Billuart.

> Duo distinguenda sunt in Episcopo, scilicet, extensio characteris seu potestas, et cura pastoralis animarum atque Ecclesiae quacum init matrimonium spirituale: ad hoc secundum requiritur consensus, non ad primum. Et hoc sensu intelligendum esse S. Thomam docent nobiles interpretes, Paludanus, Dominicus Soto, Gonet, alii.[18]

Today, all authors are in agreement in recognizing the validity of infant ordinations, including ordination to the episcopate.[19]

4. Eucharist

The documents of antiquity bear abundant evidence of the almost universal practice in the early Church, both in the East and in the West, of administering the Eucharist under both species to infants, either immediately after their baptism or on the days within the octave.[20] Mention is also made of the custom of administering the Eucharist to infants under the species of wine alone by dipping the finger into the Precious Blood and then touching it to the tongue of the child.[21]

So widespread was this custom that Cardinal De Lugo, after having cited the extant documents, concluded:

[17] *Summa Theologica, Suppl.,* q. 39, a. 2.

[18] *Summa Sancti Thomas* (Parisiis, n.d.), *Tractatus de Sacramento Ordinis,* Diss. iii, art. 3, par. 1.

[19] Cf. Cappello, *De Sacramentis,* IV, n. 357.

[20] Cappello, *De Sacramentis,* I, n. 412.

[21] Cappello, *loc. cit.*

> Constat enim ex supra adductis, in omnibus fere provinciis usum illum viguisse . . . nam in Orientali ecclesia hodie durat; in Occidentali vero seu Latina, vidimus Africam, Hispaniam, Galliam, Romam ipsam hunc morem tenuisse.[22]

The practice of administering the Eucharist to infants under one or both species is still retained in parts of the Eastern Church. It has practically disappeared among the Maronites, the Syrians, the Copts of Egypt, the Malabars, and the Rumanians. It is on the wane among the Ruthenians, but still retained by the Greeks.[23] In the West, however, more as the result of custom than of express law, a prohibition against giving the Eucharist to infants came into being from the XII century onward.[24]

This prohibition was a purely disciplinary measure to prevent the danger of irreverence and the other inevitable evils which would surely follow from the abuse of such a practice.[25]

Despite the abundant evidence of the widespread practice of infant Communion in the Church, some authors mentioned by Vazquez (1549-1604) denied that infants received the Eucharist in a sacramental and fruitful manner.[26] The majority of the authors, however, rejected this view.

> Praecipuum fundamentum desumitur ex usu antiquo Ecclesiae dandi parvulis Eucharistiam, qui certe usus licitus non fuisset, si in eis non posset suum effectum habere; sicut nec liceret dare illam catechumeno, etiamsi sit in gratia, propter eandem rationem, nec homini mortuo aut bruto, quia id esset fraudare sacramentum suo effectu; supponebant ergo patres antiqui parvulos esse capaces fructus hujus sacramenti.[27]

22 *Disputationes Scholasticae et Morales, Tractatus de Sacramento Eucharistiae,* Disp. xiii, n. 12.

23 Cappello, *De Sacramentis,* I, n. 799.

24 Coronata, *De Sacramentis,* I, n. 309.

25 De Lugo, *De Sacramentis in Genere,* Disp. ix, n. 112.

26 Vazquez, *Commentariorum ac Disputationum in Tertiam Partem Sancti Thomae Tomus II* (Lugduni, 1631), Q. 80, a. 9, disp. 212, c. 2 (hereafter cited as *Commentarii*).

27 De Lugo, *De Sacramento Eucharistiae,* Disp. xiii, n. 10.

Under the present dispensation infants continue of course to enjoy the capacity to receive the Eucharist under the divine law. However, they lack this capacity in virtue of the positive law of the Church, and even though the infants were to receive an increase of grace by its reception, nevertheless the minister of the sacrament would be guilty of a serious sacrilege.[28]

C. Infants are Incapable of Receiving Extreme Unction and Penance

It has been the constant and universal practice of the Church not to confer extreme unction upon infants. This practice has now been embodied into the Code, which declares:

> Extreme unction can be administered only to one of the faithful who, after attaining the use of reason, is in danger of death through sickness or old age.[29]

Authors are in virtual agreement that this prohibition is founded upon the dogmatic fact that infants are incapable of validly receiving extreme unction.[30]

In seeking, however, to uncover the intrinsic reasons for this incapacity, one does not find the same unanimity among the writers. As Cappello himself acknowledges, the reasons suggested by the authors are not wholly conclusive and demonstrative.[31]

In this regard one may well reproduce *in extenso* the text of Kilker (1901-1944).

> Kern seems to advance the best argument in the matter. Each sacrament, he tells us, is instituted principally for one effect, although others may follow therefrom secondarily.

[28] Coronata, *De Sacramentis,* I, n. 309.

[29] Can. 940, § 1.

[30] Cappello, *De Sacramentis,* III, n. 213; Merkelbach, *Summa Theologiae Moralis,* III, n. 704.

[31] "Quidam recentiores tenent, nullam intrinsecam rationem afferri posse, cur infantes arceantur a fructibus extremae unctionis; addunt, autem, rationes adductas ab Angelico aliisque Scholasticis non esse omnes concludentes. Quod, debita servata reverentia erga insignes Doctores, concedendum est."—Cappello, *De Sacramentis,* III (3. ed., Romae: Marietti, 1949), n. 217, 2.

> In Extreme Unction this effect is the *confortatio habitualis*, the right to every help or aid which promotes the alleviation of the soul. Now it needs no proof that an infant is altogether incapable of enjoying actual comforting of soul against the debilities caused therein by sin. However, it remains to be shown that he is also incompetent to receive the habitual comfort given by the sacrament.
>
> There is a repugnance in the very concept of giving a right which can never be used because of the want of sufficient time to come into such a position where it may be used. . . . Such a right is misnamed. Similarly it would be the lot of an infant to attain to benefits which would be of value only for the time of sickness. While sick, he could make no use of it, for he is incapable of actual spiritual alleviation. He is neither tempted nor depressed. If he recovers and reaches reason's age, his title to the supernatural aids will have vanished, for the duration of these rights is co-extensive only with the period of danger of death. As a consequence, infants become, by their utter incompetency, either active or passive, of receiving alleviation, absolutely invalid subjects of Extreme Unction.[32]

Since the proximate matter of the sacrament of penance is the contrition, confession and satisfaction of the sinner, and the remote matter is his past sins, infants are obviously incapable of receiving this sacrament.

Bonacina (ca. 1585-1631) summed up the teaching of his own time, as still reflected also in our present age, in regard to the capacity of infants for the sacraments, when he declared: "Parvuli, uti et perpetuo amentes valide *baptizantur, confirmantur, communicantur, ordinantur. . . .*"[33]

D. Intention of Infants Is Supplied

Although infants can be the recipients of certain sacraments, the authors hasten to add that these sacraments are not conferred apart from any and every intention at all. Rather, in the case of infants, in place of a personal intention an intention is supplied for them by Christ or by the Church.

[32] Kilker, *Extreme Unction*, The Catholic University of America Canon Law Studies, n. 32 (Washington, D. C.: The Catholic University of America, 1926), pp. 138-139.

[33] *Opera Omnia* (3 vols., Venetiis, 1687), Vol. I, Disp. I, *de sacramentis*, q. 6, punctum 2, n. 1 (hereafter cited as *De Sacramentis*).

> Cum tantum requirantur conditiones juxta subjecti capacitatem, parvuli autem et perpetuo amentes non sint capaces propriae intentionis, sufficit illis intentio Christi et Ecclesiae.[34]

Elsewhere St. Alphonsus again wrote that the intention was supplied for infants: "In infantibus nulla requiritur intentio, cum suppleat in eis intentio Christi vel Ecclesiae,"[35] but Gaudé, in his edition of St. Alphonsus, limited the application of this somewhat—"saltem pro Baptismo et Confirmatione,"—without citing reasons for this limitation.[36]

Martin of Braga (d. 580) already spoke of this intention in regard to a mother with child, in which case, he said, a separate act of the will for baptism was required for the mother, another for the child. "Nihil participat," he said, "in hoc mater infanti, qui nascitur, propterea, quod unicuique propria voluntas in confessione monstratur."[37] The Gloss to this same canon indicates that there is a distinction between the will of the mother for baptism and that of the child, and it is stated that the will of each must be sought out. "Nec in hoc aliquid habet commune cum filio. Nam alia est voluntas matris, alia filii, et ideo cujuslibet eorum voluntas in confessione est inquirendus."[38]

This will for baptism found its external expression in the offering of the child for baptism by its parents or sponsors. "Parvuli intelliguntur baptizati in fide parentum et patrinorum."[39] If, however, the parents were infidels, or if they had a false or materialistic concept of the sacrament which they requested for their child, the validity of the sacrament was not thereby impaired, for then the child was offered, not simply by the sponsors, but by the entire society of the faithful, which is the Church.

> Offeruntur quippe parvuli ad percipiendam spiritualem gratiam, non tam ab iis, quorum gestantur manibus (quam-

[34] St. Alphonsus, *Theologia Moralis,* Lib. VI, n. 78; cf. also Lacroix, *Theologia Moralis,* Lib. VI, n. 163.

[35] *Theologia Moralis,* Lib. VI, n. 80.

[36] *Ibid.,* note 78 b.

[37] C. 116, D. IV, *de cons.*

[38] *Glossa Ord.* ad c. 116, D. IV, *de cons.*

[39] Hostiensis, *Summa Aurea* (Lugduni, 1570), Lib. III, tit. 42, n. 8.

> vis et ab ipsis, si et ipsi boni fideles sunt), quam ab universa societate sanctorum et fidelium. . . . Tota ergo hoc mater ecclesia, quae in sanctis est, facit." [40]

Even if the parents in bringing their child to the baptismal font were motivated by a desire to find a remedy to preserve the health of the child, or a means to regain its health, nevertheless the sacrament was valid, for the child did not remain without regeneration for the reason simply that its parents lacked all intention or desire for its spiritual regeneration.

> Non illud te moveat, quod quidam non ea fide ad baptismum percipiendum parvulos ferunt, ut gratia spiritali ad vitam regenerentur aeternam; sed hoc eos putant remedio temporalem retinere vel recipere sanitatem. Non enim propterea non regenerantur, quia non ab istis hac intentione offeruntur.[41]

Whence, then, came the correct and proper intention for the sacrament in such a case? The Glossator answered that it came from the Church, which itself offered these children for baptism. "Intelliguntur offerri ab ipsa Ecclesia." [42]

It was also the teaching of St. Thomas that the intention of infants for the sacrament was supplied by their sponsors or by the Church. He declared that "they can be said to intend, not by their own act of intention, but by the act of those who bring them to be baptized." [43]

E. No Intention Is Required from the Perpetually Insane

There are, of course, the unfortunate cases of those individuals who, though adults in the point of years, yet remain incapable of a normal mental activity. These are the insane, the *amentes*. Clearly, they, like infants, are incapable at any precise moment of eliciting an intention. The question which must now be answered is whether they are therefore to be excluded from the reception of the sacraments.

40 C. 129, D. IV, *de cons.*

41 C. 33, D. IV, *de cons.*

42 *Glossa Ord.* ad c. 33, D. IV, *de cons.*, s.v. *intentionem.*

43 *Summa Theologica.* III, q. 68, a. 9, ad 1.

1. A Distinction Must Be Made Among the Insane

In regard to the insane and their intention for the sacraments, it is first of all necessary to make a distinction between those who have been insane since their birth, and those who have become such only after having first enjoyed the use of reason. This distinction was already made by St. Thomas.

> Respondeo dicendum quod circa amentes et furiosos est distinguendum. Quidam enim sunt a nativitate tales, nulla habentes lucida intervalla, in quibus etiam nullus usus rationis apparet. . . . Alii vero sunt amentes, qui ex sana mente quam habuerunt prius, in amentiam inciderunt.[44]

This distinction also found a place among the commentators.

> Quid de furiosis baptizatis? *Si semper fuit furiosus,* tenet baptismus, nam et tales parvulis et dormientibus aequiparantur. . . . *Si vero incidat in furorem* vel incipiat quis dormire. . . .[45]

This same distinction is embodied in the present Code legislation on baptism. Canon 745, § 2, 1°, states:

> Under the name of children or infants, in accordance with the norm of canon 88, § 3, come all those who have not yet attained the use of reason, and to be regarded as in a class with them are those who have been insane from infancy, no matter what their age.

A particular application of this canon is to be found in canon 754, § 1, which treats of those who are insane or mad, when this condition has existed from the time of their birth, or at least from a time prior to their attainment of the use of reason.

2. The Insane from Birth Are to Be Treated as Infants

Canon 745, § 2, 1°, declares that in regard to baptism those who are insane from birth are to be treated as and regarded the same as infants. More specifically, all in regard to baptism, canon 754, § 1, provides:

> Those who are insane or mad shall not be baptized unless they were in this condition from birth, or from a time prior

[44] *Summa Theologica,* III, q. 68, a. 12, in corp.

[45] Hostiensis, *Summa Aurea,* Lib. III, tit. 42, n.

to their attainment of the use of reason; and then they are to be baptized as infants.

Not only in regard to baptism, but also in the reception of the other sacraments as well, the rules that apply for infants are to be applied for those who are insane from birth. De Lugo states it in this way:

> Quod dicitur de parvulis, dici debet de perpetuis amentibus, qui numquam usum rationis habuerunt, et idcirco aequiparantur parvulis quoad omnia.[46]

Thus the perpetually insane are capable of validly receiving baptism, confirmation, Holy Eucharist, and Holy Orders.[47] They are incapable of receiving extreme unction and penance.[48] Since the perpetually insane are equally unable with infants to elicit an intention, their intention is also supplied by Christ and by his Church.

> Cum tantum requirantur conditiones juxta subjecti capacitatem, parvuli autem et perpetuo amentes non sint capaces propriae intentionis, sufficit illis intentio Christi et Ecclesiae.[49]

[46] *De Sacramentis in Genere,* Disp. ix, n. 112.

[47] ". . . perpetuo amentes valide baptizantur, confirmantur, communicantur, ordinantur. . . ."—Bonacina, *De Sacramentis,* q. 6, punctum 2, n. 1.

[48] Pruemmer, *Manuale Theologiae Moralis,* III, n. 87; III, n. 580.

[49] St. Alphonsus, *Theologia Moralis,* Lib. VI, n. 78.

CHAPTER III

AN INTENTION IS REQUIRED OF ADULTS FOR THE RECEPTION OF THE SACRAMENTS

A. Definition of Adult

"It is admitted by all Christians that an intention is required in the adult recipient of the sacraments."[1] Now, it is necessary to determine more precisely who is an adult in the matter of the administration of the sacraments. Canon 745, § 2, places all prospective subjects for the sacrament of baptism into one or the other of two categories. They are either infants or they are adults. Considered as infants are all those who have not yet reached the age of seven, at which time the jurisprudence of the Church has judged that the use of reason, and consequently adulthood, begins.

> Pueri quinquennes sunt omnino infantibus seu parvulis accensendi, ex quo tempus infantiae, ab utroque iure, primo humanae vitae septennio definitur. Idque etiam, quod ad baptismum attinet, huiusce S. Congregationis documentis roboratur.[2]

Also included in this category of infants are those who are perpetually insane, those who have never possessed the use of reason.[3] This centuries-long jurisprudence finds expression in the Code in canon 745 § 1, 1°, which states:

> Parvulorum seu infantium nomine veniunt ad normam canonis 88, § 3, qui nondum rationis usum adepti sunt eis-

[1] Leeming, *Principles of Sacramental Theology*, p. 495.

[2] S. C. S. Off., instr. (ad Archiep. Portus Principis), 5 sept. 1877; *Codicis Iuris Canonici Fontes*, cura Emi Petri Card. Gasparri editi, 9 vols., Romae (postea Civitate Vaticana): Typis Polyglottis Vaticanis, 1923-1939 (Vols. VII-IX, ed. cura et studio Emi Justiniani Card. Seredi), n. 1053; hereafter cited as *Fontes.*

[3] "Si semper fiat furiosus, tenet baptismus, nam et tales parvulis et dormientibus aequiparantur. . . ."—Hostiensis, *Summa Aurea*, Lib. III, tit. 42, n. 9.

demque accensentur amentes ab infantia, in quavis aetate constituti.

All others not included in this classification of infants are to be regarded as adults. All of these latter have at one time or another enjoyed the use of reason. Hence this class includes all those who actually here and now have the use of reason. It includes as well those who are now insane, but who once did have the use of reason, though they are now temporarily deprived of it, as a result, for example, of excessive drinking, of the use of narcotics, of coma, of frenzy, etc. Briefly, then, anyone who has at any time had the use of reason is considered an adult, and for these an intention is always necessary. Those who have never had the use of reason, no matter what may be their age, are infants, and for them no intention is either necessary or even possible.

What has been said here in regard to baptism will apply equally well to the other sacraments under consideration, since these principles look to and consider the common generic nature of the sacraments.

B. The Free Reception of the Sacraments Is Befitting

The necessity of any intention cannot be demonstrated from the nature of the sacraments themselves. If God had so chosen and so willed, He could have instituted the sacraments in such a way that they could be received by men apart from all freedom or consent on their part. From the teaching and the practice of the Church, however, it is known that God has not chosen to act in this way, but rather insists on man's free consent if he is to be the beneficiary of God's grace. The basis, then, of the requirement of an intention lies in the free will of God himself.[4]

Once it has been shown, however, from the testimony of the past that it has always been the practice of the Church to demand an intention from the recipient of the sacrament, then the fittingness of such a requirement can be clearly shown.

St. Augustine clearly expressed the need for our co-operation in the salvation of our own souls in his famous words:

[4] Connell, *De Sacramentis Ecclesiae*, n. 60.

> Qui ergo fecit te sine te, non te justificat sine te. Ergo fecit nescientem, justificat volentem.[5]

St. Thomas wrote in a similar fashion. He argued thus to the need of an intention:

> Deus autem movet omnia secundum modum uniuscuiusque. . . . Unde et homines ad justitiam movet secundum conditionem naturae humanae. Homo autem secundum propriam naturam habet quod sit liberi arbitrii. Et ideo in eo qui habet usum liberi arbitrii, non fit motio a Deo ad justitiam absque motu liberi arbitrii.[6]

In conclusion, the Council of Trent may be cited. It proclaimed the general principle that justification takes place *"per voluntariam susceptionem gratiae et donorum."*

> This disposition or preparation is followed by justification itself, which is not only a remission of sins but also the sanctification and renewal of the inward man through the voluntary reception of the grace and gifts whereby an unjust man becomes just. . . .[7]

The doctrine concerning the real necessity of an intention for the adult recipient of the sacrament has never been explicitly defined. However, this teaching must be regarded as theologically certain, since it finds ample support and foundation in the ancient traditions of the Church as well as in its centuries-long practice.[8]

C. The Church Insists on Freedom in the Reception of the Sacraments

The great importance which the Church has always attached to a free and voluntary reception of the sacraments can be seen in its constant insistence that the sacraments are not to be conferred forcibly upon those who are unwilling to receive them. This is particularly true in regard to the sacraments of baptism

[5] Sermo 169, c. 11—Migne, *Patrologiae Cursus Completus, Series Latina* (221 vols., Parisiis, 1844-1864), XXXVIII, 925.

[6] *Summa Theologica,* Ia-IIae, q. 113, a. 3.

[7] Conc. Trident., Sess. VI, *de justificatione,* cap. 7—Mansi, XXXIII, 34-35; Schroeder, *The Canons and Decrees,* p. 33.

[8] Connell, *De Sacramentis Ecclesiae,* n. 60.

and Holy Orders. Baptism introduces the recipient into the society of the Church; Holy Orders brings with it the position of leadership in that same Church. Since they confer a character, these sacraments possess a greater degree of permanency than some of the others. Not only, then, do these sacraments confer a more or less permanent status in the Church, but they bring with them concomitantly some serious obligations. Hence greater and more serious problems can be reasonably expected in their regard, and accordingly greater insistence is placed upon freedom in their reception.

Various "cases of conscience" arose in the history of the Church about the question of the intention of the recipient. Certain monarchs had forced their people to follow the royal lead and to accept baptism. One of these was the Visigothic king, Sisebut (d. 621). The IV Council of Toledo (633) declared that in the future no force was to be employed in the bringing of the Jews into the Church.

> De Judaeis autem praecepit sancta synodus, nemini deinceps vim ad credendum inferre . . . non vi, sed libera arbitrii facultate ut convertantur suadendi sunt, non potius impellendi.[9]

A similar admonition was issued five centuries later by Clement III (1187-1191), when he forbade the use of force to compel Jews to accept baptism.

> Statuimus ut nullus Christianus invitos vel nolentes Judaeos ad baptismum per violentiam venire compellat. . . .[10]

Nevertheless, it was necessary for one of his successors in the papacy, again five centuries later, to issue a similar injunction to such as were employed in the mission activities of the Church.

> Monentur ecclesiastici, tum seculares, tum regulares, caeterique qui ethnicorum conversionibus dant operam, ut illos non vexationibus, pollicitationibus, aut vi, sed verbi Dei praedicatione, et bonorum operum exemplo ad baptismum inducant.[11]

[9] C. 5, D. XLV.

[10] C. 9, X, *de Judaeis, Saracenis, et eorum servis,* V, 6.

[11] Alexander VII, const. *Sacrosancti,* 18 ian. 1658, § 2, 15°—*Fontes,* n. 235.

Despite its divine assurance regarding the universal necessity of membership in the Church as well as the universal necessity of baptism, nevertheless the Church at the same time has always insisted on the freedom each man enjoys to accept or reject the divine beneficence.

Hence canon 1351 provides: *"Ad amplexandam fidem catholicam nemo invitus cogatur."* The Code also insists that baptism is to be conferred only when the recipient is willing to accept it.

> Adultus, nisi sciens et volens probeque instructus, ne baptizetur.[12]

A similar insistence upon complete freedom and liberty, and the rejection of every form of compulsion, is to be found in the jurisprudence of the Church in regard to Holy Orders. Gratian in the rubric of a decree taken from Pope Simplicius had stated: *"Non est aliquis invitus ad episcopatum pertrahendus,"*[13] even though, as can be ascertained from the comment of the Glossator at this point, the validity of such an episcopal consecration was not called into question.[14]

In the early Church deacons played a most important rôle in the administration of diocesan affairs. To them were entrusted the care of the poor and the needy, the administration of the temporal possessions of the diocese, and the handling of its business affairs, as well as certain spiritual functions, including the task of baptizing and the distribution of the Eucharist to the sick.[15] Because of their skill and experience in practical affairs, they were often chosen to succeed the bishop who had appointed them. Gradually the deacons gained even greater administrative powers, which overshadowed those of the priests. Many deacons, therefore, refused to be ordained to the priesthood, preferring to retain their more influential positions.

Accordingly, it was provided that, if some of the deacons

[12] Canon 752, § 1.

[13] C. 7, D. LXXIV.

[14] "Licet quis coactus ordinetur, tamen recipit ordinem."—*Glossa Ord.* ad c. 7, D. LXXIV, s.v. *honorem.*

[15] Zeiger, *Historia Iuris Canonici,* II (Romae: Apud Aedes Universitatis Gregorianae, 1947), p. 45.

should refuse to be promoted to the priesthood, they were not to be compelled. Rather, worthy candidates were to be chosen from the lower clergy.[16]

On a local level the III Council of Orleans (538) prescribed that, if any bishop presumed to ordain a man who was unwilling and opposed to his ordination, such a bishop *ipso facto* incurred a suspension from saying Mass for an entire year.[17]

D. Intention Is Necessary for the Reception of Baptism

The Sacred Congregation for the Propagation of the Faith in an instruction to the Vicar Apostolic of Siam in 1830 cited the canons of the III Council of Carthage (397) and of the I Council of Orange (441) in proof of the necessity of an intention for the reception of baptism on the part of adults.

> Etiam in adultis aliqua intentio necessaria est ad valorem sacramenti quod recipiunt; quod declaratum fuit in Conc. Carthag. III and Araus. I. Haec de necessariis ad valorem Baptismi si hic consideratur in generica sacramenti ratione.[18]

The III Council of Carthage (397), while repeating the earlier provisions of the Council of Hippo (393), had ruled that, in the event that a person was at the time incapable of expressing his desire for baptism, nevertheless he was not always to be excluded from receiving the sacrament. The minister of the sacrament under such circumstances could rely on the testimony of friends to the effect that the dying man wished to be baptized or to be absolved.

[16] "Quapropter, quia invitos fieri ecclesiastica moderatio gravitasque non patitur, ut ex nolentibus fiant volentes ordinatio illa potest perficere, si quos habes in acolitis, vel subdiaconibus maturiores aetate, et quorum sit vita probabilis, hos in presbyterium studeas promovere. . . ."—C. 9, D. LXXIV; Jaffé, *Regesta Pontificum Romanorum ab condita Ecclesia ad annum post Christ natum* MCXCVIII (*2. ed. correctam et auctam auspiciis Gulielmi Wattenbach, curaverunt F. Kaltenbrunner, P. Ewald, S. Loewenfeld,* 2 vols., Lipsiae, 1885-1888), n. 668 (hereafter cited as Jaffé).

[17] "Episcopus, qui invitum aut reclamantem ordinare praesumpserit, annuali penitentiae subditus missas facere non praesumat."—C. 1, D. LXXIV.

[18] S. C. de Prop. Fide., instr. (ad Vic. Ap. Siam), 23 iun. 1830—*Fontes,* n. 4748.

> Aegrotantes, si pro se respondere non possunt, cum voluntatis eorum testimonium sui dixerint, baptizentur. Similiter et de penitentibus agendum est.[19]

The I Council of Orange (441) also acknowledged that the testimony regarding a previous request for baptism or penance when given by friends would suffice, as did a simple nod of the head.

> Similiter subito obmutescens baptizari aut penitentiam accipere potest, si voluntatis praeteritae testimonium aliorum verbis habet, aut praesentis in suo nutu.[20]

Thus, even in the most extreme case, the minister was expected to first ascertain whether the dying person had expressed in an external manner his desire to receive the sacraments.

In his decretal letter *Maiores*, Pope Innocent III (1198-1216) authoritatively treated the question of the necessity of an intention for the sacraments. According to Innocent III there were those who denied that an intention was necessary for certain of the sacraments. Among those sacraments they enumerated baptism, Orders, and others like them, sacraments which, they said, obtain their effect in and of themselves (*per se*), an expression explained by the Glossator as meaning "Without the consent of the recipient."[21]

In support of their contention they argued from the generally acknowledged fact that the insane, and persons in a state of coma, and also the unwilling, even those who positively reject the sacrament, all receive at least the sacramental character, if not the accompanying grace of the sacrament.

> Sunt autem nonnulli, qui dicunt, quod sacramenta, quae per se sortiuntur effectum, ut baptismus et ordo ceteraque similia, non solum dormientibus et amentibus, sed invitis etiam et contradicentibus, etsi non quantum ad rem, quantum tamen ad characterem conferuntur, cum non solum parvuli qui non consentiunt, sed et ficti, qui quamvis non ore, corde tamen dissentiunt, recipiant sacramentum.[22]

[19] C. 75, D. IV, *de cons.*

[20] C. 7, D. XXVI, q. 6.

[21] "Absque consensu accipientis."—*Glossa Ord.* ad. c. 3, X, *de baptismo et eius effectu,* III, 42, s.v., *quae per se sortiuntur.*

[22] C. 3, X, *de baptismo et eius effectu,* III, 42.

This view, which denied the necessity of an intention for the recipient, found expression in the Gloss to this very decretal of Innocent III. "In baptismo non requiritur intentio baptizati, sed baptizantis." [23]

The same doctrine is found elsewhere in the Gloss. "Ad hoc dico quod si baptizans intendit baptizare, qualemcumque intentionem baptizatus habeat, recipit sacramentum." [24]

According to Hostiensis (d. 1271), the famous commentator Huguccio (d. 1210) was an exponent of this view, holding that it was only the intention of the minister that was demanded for a valid baptism, regardless of what might be the intention of those who offered the person, or even of the one who presented himself for baptism.

> Secundum Huguccio requiritur quod baptizans intendat baptizare, alias nihil agitur, sed non requiritur intentio offerentium vel baptizatorum.[25]

The response of Innocent III leaves no room for doubt. He rejected the opinion which denied the necessity of an intention. He pointed out how such a view in its practical consequences was contrary to the constant practice of the Church. In this connection he cited the provisions of the IV Council of Toledo (633), which forbade forced conversions and baptism among the Jews.[26]

Next, the Pontiff proceeded to indicate where he considered the solution of this problem lay, namely, by making a distinction between the various degrees of compulsion and force. "Propter quod inter invitum et invitum, coactum et coactum, alii non absurde distinguunt." [27] As long as the person was conditionally willing (*conditionaliter volens*), this voluntary consent mixed with an involuntary element could suffice for the validity of the sacrament.

Finally, the Pope showed clearly that a habitual intention sufficed for the reception of the sacraments. Accordingly, the

[23] *Glossa Ord.* ad. c. 3, X, *de baptismo et eius effectu,* III, 42, s.v. *perdurare.*

[24] *Glossa Ord.* ad c. 31, D. IV, *de cons.,* s.v. *implorandum.*

[25] Hostiensis, *Summa Aurea,* Lib. III, tit. 42, n. 16.

[26] Cf. *supra,* p. 39.

[27] C. 3, X, *de baptismo et eius effectu,* III, 42.

sick in a state of coma, the insane, or also those who were asleep, could receive the sacraments validly, if they had formed such an intention at some earlier time in their lives. Moreover, he showed that without such an intention the valid and fruitful reception of the sacrament was not possible.

> Ille vero, qui numquam consentit, sed penitus contradicit, nec rem, nec characterem suscipit sacramenti.[28]

The decretalists, in commenting on the teaching of Innocent III, frequently took for granted the necessity of an intention, and simply proceeded to discuss the practical problems which this raised. Many, therefore, sought to determine what kind of intention was required, especially in the more difficult cases.

However, some of the writers did state explicitly the necessity of an intention. The Glossator, e.g., stated: *"Intentio baptizati et baptizantis exigitur."* [29] Panormitanus (1386-1453) and Innocent IV (1243-1254) were equally explicit in stating this requirement, as was Joannes Andreae (1272-1348).[30]

The documents of the Holy See provide incontrovertible evidence that an intention is to be regarded as so necessary for the recipient of the sacraments that without it the sacrament is invalidly conferred. This is the clear teaching of the Instruction to the Vicar Apostolic of Siam.

> Etiam in adultis aliqua intentio necessaria est ad valorem sacramenti quod recipiunt; . . . . Haec de necessariis ad valorem Baptismi si hic consideratur in generica sacramenti ratione.[31]

[28] C. 3, X, *de baptismo et eius effectu,* III, 42.

[29] *Glossa Ord.* ad c. 46, C. I, q. 1, s.v. *ebrius.*

[30] "Nam requiritur intentio utriusque."—Panormitanus, *Commentaria in Quinque Libros Decretalium* (Venetiis, 1588), Lib. III, tit. 42, c. 6, n. 5 (hereafter cited as Panormitanus); "Et non quod licet intentio baptizantis et baptizati impediat sacramentum, tamen intentio patrinorum numquam impedit."—Innocentius IV, *In Quinque libros Decretalium Commentaria* (Venetiis, 1570), Lib. III, tit. 42, c. 1, n. 8 (hereafter cited as Innocentius IV); "Valet baptismus dummodo baptismum conferre et conferri intendat." —Joannes Andreae, *In Tertium Librum Decretalium Novella Commentaria* (Venetiis, 1581), Lib. III, tit. 42, c. 2, n. 3.

[31] S. C. de Prop. Fide, instr. (ad Vic. Ap. Siam), 23 iun. 1830—*Fontes,* n. 4748.

The same doctrine appears in several passages in a later instruction sent to the Vicar Apostolic of Tche Kiang in 1860.

> Necessario requiritur intentio seu voluntas suscipiendi hoc sacramentum, eaque deficiente, non imprimitur in adulto baptismatis character.

Elsewhere in the same instruction it is stated:

> Intentio vero necessario est ad illud valide consequendum; qui baptizatur absque voluntate sacramentum suscipiendi, nec licite nec valide baptizatur.[32]

Finally, a doubt was proposed to the Holy Office whether a missionary could baptize an adult Mohammedan, who supposedly was in good faith, once he had lost consciousness. In a response whose tenor recalls the previously cited canons of the III Council of Carthage (397) and the I Council of Orange (441), the Holy Office replied that even under such extreme circumstances inquiry was to be made whether the dying man had previously by some sign indicated a desire for the sacrament.

> Si antea dederint signa velle baptizari, vel in praesenti statu aut nutu aut alio modo eandem dispositionem ostenderint, baptizari posse sub conditione, quatenus tamen missionarius, cunctis rerum adiunctis inspectis, ita prudenter iudicaverit.[33]

A similar insistence upon searching out the presence of an intention even in those who are dying while destitute of their senses is found in canon 752, § 3.

> Quod si baptismum ne petere quidem queat, sed vel antea vel in praesenti statu manifestaverit aliquo probabili modo intentionem illum suscipiendi, baptizandus est sub conditione;

E. An Intention Is Necessary for the Reception of the Other Sacraments

Since the reception of baptism brings with it so many obligations on the part of the new Christian, many practical doubts

[32] S. C. S. Off., instr. (ad Vic. Ap. Tche-Kiang), 1 aug. 1860.

[33] S. C. S. Off., 30 mart. 1898, ad 3—*Fontes*, n. 1197. This response merely repeats a previous reply to the Bishop of Perth on September 18, 1850, ad 2—*Fontes*, n. 912.

and consequently many official documents are to be expected in regard to the necessity of an intention for the reception of this sacrament. It is to be anticipated that not so many will be found in regard to the other sacraments.

The Holy Office in a letter dated May 10, 1703, declared:

> Non est pariter conferendum Sacramentum Extremae Unctionis neophyto moribundo, quem missionarius capacem Baptismi credidit, nisi saltem idem habeat aliquam intentionem recipiendi sacram Unctionem in beneficium animae, pro mortis tempore, ordinatam.[34]

A similar response of the Holy Office in 1861 included confirmation as well.

> Nec conferendum sacramentum confirmationis nec Extremae Unctionis illis neophytis moribundis . . . nisi saltem habeant aliquam intentionem percipiendi Confirmationem ad robur animae suae adiiciendum et recipiendi S. Unctionem in beneficium animae pro mortis tempore ordinatam.[35]

Appeal may also be made to the text of the decretal *Maiores* of Innocent III, where the opinion of those who claimed that baptism, Orders, and other sacraments like them could be received *"absque consensu accipientis,"* was expressly rejected by the Pope.

In writing of the necessity of an intention for all the sacraments, St. Thomas taught:

> In baptismo baptizatus duo recipit, scilicet, sacramentum et rem sacramenti. Sed ad haec duo recipienda non requiritur aliquid causans ex parte recipientis, sed solum impedimentum removens; quod quidem impedimentum nihil aliud est quam voluntas contraria alteri praedictorum, et ideo in adultis, et in habentibus usum rationis, in quibus potest esse contraria voluntas actu vel habitu, requiritur contritio, sive devotio ad percipiendam rem sacramenti, et intentio vel voluntas ad recipiendum sacramentum.[36]

[34] S. C. S. Off. (Quebec), 10 maii 1703—*Fontes,* n. 765.

[35] S. C. S. Off. (Techely Meridio-Oriental.), 10 apr. 1861—*Fontes,* n. 965.

[36] *Commentum in Quatuor Libros Sententiarum,* In IV, D. VI, q. 1, a. 2, q. 3, sol. 3. Billot (1846-1931) cited this text, but in a somewhat different form. Cf. *De Ecclesiae Sacramentis,* I (7. ed., Romae, 1931), p. 206.

In this St. Thomas is followed by all theologians and canonists.

> Communis et vera sententia theologorum tenet requiri ad valorem sacramenti consensum positivum adulti qui illud recipit.[37]

F. Neutral Intention Does Not Suffice

Opposed to this common teaching is the singular opinion advanced by Cajetan (1469-1534). He based himself upon the words of Innocent III as expressed in the decretal *Maiores,* especially on the words which close the discussion concerning the baptism of imbeciles and the insane. *"Tunc ergo characterem sacramentalis imprimit operatio, cum obicem voluntatis contrariae non invenit obsistentem."* [38] From these words Cajetan argued that in theory the absence simply of a contrary intention in the case of an unconscious dying person would not preclude the reception of the sacrament. It was his view that for the validity of baptism a positive act of consent was not required, but that simply a negative or neutral intention was all that was needed. St. Alphonsus explained this neutral intention thus: *"Nempe quod non consentiat neque dissentiat."* [39]

Thus, in the opinion of Cajetan, the sacrament of baptism was always validly administered as long as no contrary intention was present in the recipient, and despite all lack of any positive desire for its reception. Practically, however, Cajetan admitted that it would be a most rare occasion for an adult to approach for the reception of baptism and yet not have a positive intention to receive the sacrament.

This unique opinion of Cajetan was rejected and refuted by many later authors. Vazquez, for one, disagreed with Cajetan on the possible frequency of such a neutral intention, and, though he misrepresented somewhat the position of Cajetan on this matter, he still rightly pointed to the not unusual cases wherein a person has fallen into a state of permanent insanity when beforehand he had never thought of or heard about baptism.[40]

[37] De Lugo, *De Sacramentis in Genere,* Disp. ix, n. 115.

[38] C. 3, X, *de baptismo et eius effectu,* III, 32, *in fine.*

[39] *Theologia Moralis,* Lib. VI, n. 81.

[40] Vazquez, *Commentarii,* q. 69, a. 10, disp. 157, c. 2, n. 4.

Cajetan's opinion received a severe setback when Benedict XIV in an instruction on baptism addressed to the Vice-Regent of Rome in 1747 evidently subscribed to the other teaching, which required a positive intention for the validity of the sacrament.[41] Finally, an examination of the text of Innocent III reveals that the decretal's words "plainly refer to the case of the mentally deranged at the moment of death, who might have had lucid intervals. His solution was that they are to be baptized or not according to one's judgment as to their frame of mind in their last lucid interval; and if they are effectively infants they may be baptized."[42]

[41] Benedictus XIV, ep. *Postremo mense,* 28 febr. 1747, n. 46—*Fontes,* n. 377.

[42] Leeming, *Principles of Sacramental Theology,* p. 496.

CHAPTER IV

A HABITUAL INTENTION IS REQUIRED BUT ALSO SUFFICES FOR THE RECEPTION OF THE SACRAMENTS

A. Early Canonical Sources Indicate That a Habitual Intention Is Sufficient

In the preceding chapter the necessity of some kind of intention on the part of the recipient of the sacraments was demonstrated. It now remains to ascertain more precisely what kind of intention is required and will suffice. It is known that to confer the sacraments validly the minister must possess at least a virtual intention.[1]

The question arises, then, whether the same virtual intention is required of the recipient of the sacrament as well, or whether some lesser intention will suffice.

Beginning with the closing years of the fourth century, one finds that it was the unbroken practice of the Church to confer at least certain sacraments upon those of her children who were dying and were destitute of their senses. The III Council of Carthage (397), therefore, provided that in those cases wherein the sick were unable to speak for themselves at the time of the priest's arrival the word of others as to their desire to be baptized could be accepted and they might be given the sacrament. Similar provisions were enacted in regard to the sacrament of penance.

> Aegrotantes, si pro se respondere non possunt, cum voluntatis eorum testimonium sui dixerint, baptizentur. Similiter et de penitentibus agendum est.[2]

In many cases the sick to whom these two sacraments were to be administered on the basis of the testimony of others as to their previous desire were incapable of possessing an actual or a virtual intention. Such intentions presuppose a present actual

[1] Noldin, *Summa Theologiae Moralis,* III, n. 21 (2).

[2] C. 75, D. IV, *de cons.*

possession of one's faculties of intellect and will. Hence, such persons were capable of having no more than a habitual intention. Because of their earlier desire to be baptized or to be absolved, manifested in the presence of others, the Council judged that this desire to receive the sacrament had not been revoked, and accordingly continued to perdure at least habitually. Therefore, it can be seen from the provisions of this canon that the Council's fathers were of the belief that such a habitual intention proved sufficient for the sacrament, at least in this hour of extreme need.

In the following year (398) the African bishops, meeting in the IV Council of Carthage, again made provision for the administration of penance to one who had earlier indicated his desire for absolution in the presence of others, but who had afterwards lapsed into unconsciousness or frenzy before the arrival of a priest. Upon the testimony of those who had heard him ask for the sacrament, he might be absolved, and in imminent danger of death the Eucharist too might be granted to him.

> Is qui penitentiam in infirmitate petit, si casu dum ad eum sacerdos invitatus venit, oppressus infirmitate obmutuerit vel in phrenesim conversus fuerit, dent testimonium qui eum audierunt et accipiat penitentiam; et si continuo creditur moriturus, reconcilietur per manus impositionem et infudatur ori eius Eucharistia.[3]

Similar provisions can be found in the canons of the I Council of Orange (441), held on the opposite shore of the Mediterranean a few decades later. The Council of Orange also indicated that, when the sick person no longer was capable of making a formal request for the sacrament, the word of his friends in regard to a previous intention could be accepted. Moreover, the same procedure, it said, should be observed in regard to the insane.

> Similiter subito obmutescens baptizari aut penitentiam accipere potest, si voluntatis praeteritae testimonium aliorum verbis habet, aut praesentis in suo nutu. Amentibus etiam quaecumque pietatis sunt, sunt conferenda.[4]

[3] C. 8, C. XXVI, q. 6; this is canon 76 of the IV Council of Carthage and is found in Mansi, III, 957.

[4] C. 7, C. XXVI, q. 6.

Again, the persons contemplated in this canon were capable of having no more than a habitual intention, but this was judged sufficient by the fathers of the Council for the valid reception of baptism and penance.

That this was the practice in Rome is apparent from a letter of Pope Leo the Great (440-461), in which he set forth the identical doctrine as the councils in regard to the administration of the sacrament of penance.

> At si aliqua vi aegritudinis ita fuerint aggravati, ut quod paulo ante poscebant, sub praesentia sacerdotis significare non valeant, testimonia eis fidelium circumstantium prodesse debebunt, ut simul et poenitentiae et reconciliationis beneficium consequatur.[5]

B. Later Pre-Code Sources Teach That a Habitual Intention Is Sufficient

The doctrine of the oft-cited decretal *Maiores* of Innocent III was in accord with the earlier practice. In this decretal the Pope pointed out very clearly that it was the will which the person had before he became ill, or before he fell into insanity, which had to be considered. This will, this intention, continued to exist. It continued despite the fact that the person was no longer in possession of the use of reason. Thus, if earlier the person had the intention of refusing to be baptized, then the later administration, namely when he had become insane or otherwise was destitute of his senses, made the conferring of the sacrament to be invalid. This was true, not because an actual or virtual intention was required, but simply because the intention not to be baptized continued to perdure. It was this habitual intention not to receive the sacrament that became the cause of the invalidity.[6]

On the other hand, if these persons had shown some desire of being baptized, most especially if they had been numbered among the ranks of the catechumens, then, though asleep or insane, they could validly receive baptism. In their case too, then, though

[5] Ep. 108—Mansi, VI, 211.

[6] "Dormientes et amentes, si priusquam amentiam incurrerent aut dormirent, in contradictione persisterent, quia in eis intelligitur contradictionis propositum perdurare etsi fuerint sic immersi, characterem non suscipiunt sacramenti."—C. 3, X, *de baptismo et eius effectu,* III, 42.

they were incapable of either the actual or the virtual intention, they were capable of a habitual intention. Thus, it was the intention to be baptized, as previously made, that continued to perdure, and then rendered the subject fit and capable of receiving baptism validly. This teaching represented the considered custom and practice of the Roman Church under these circumstances to baptize those who were in danger of death.[7]

Pope Benedict XIV, in an instruction on baptism addressed to the Vice-Regent of Rome, cited with approval the canon of the III Council of Carthage (397), the while he declared that a baptism conferred upon one who had requested it before falling into insanity, or before falling asleep, would be valid.

> Hic casus ad eos spectat qui ante furorem vel somnum Baptismum petunt, accipiunt vero dum aut insania vexantur aut somno indulgent, et hoc genus hominum valide baptizatum dicitur. . . .[8]

Finally, a response of the Holy Office, given first in 1850, and repeated in 1898, allowed at least the conditional baptism of an adult Mohammedan, though destitute of his senses, provided that he had given some external sign of at least a probable desire to receive baptism.[9]

C. The Code and the Roman Ritual Teach That a Habitual Intention Is Sufficient

The present Code in several places recognizes the sufficiency of a habitual intention. In regard to baptism, canon 752, § 3, provides:

> Quod si baptismum ne petere quidem queat, sed vel antea vel in praesenti statu manifestaverit aliquo probabili modo intentionem illum suscipiendi, baptizandus est sub conditione.

[7] "Si prius catechumeni exstitissent, et habuissent propositum baptizandi, characterem suscipiunt sacramenti; unde tales in necessitatis articulo consuevit ecclesia baptizare."—C. 3, X, *de baptismo et eius effectu*, III, 42.

[8] Ep. *Postremo mense*, 28 febr. 1747, n. 46—*Fontes*, n. 377.

[9] "Si antea dederint signa velle baptizari, vel in praesenti statu aut nutu aut alio modo eandem dispositionem ostenderint, baptizari posse sub conditione, ..."—S. C. S. Off. (Perth.), 18 sept. 1850, ad 2; 30 mart. 1898, ad 3—*Fontes*, n. 912.

Such a habitual intention is declared to be sufficient for the valid baptism of the insane as well in canon 754, § 3.

> Baptizentur quoque [amentes], imminente periculo mortis, si, antequam insanirent, suscipiendi baptismi desiderium ostenderint.

Similar provisions are to be found in canon 754, § 4, in regard to those who are afflicted with delirium or who are in a coma when they too are in the danger of death.

Finally, canon 943 acknowledges the sufficiency of a habitual intention for extreme unction.

> Infirmis autem qui, cum suae mentis compotes essent, illud saltem implicite petierunt aut verisimiliter petiissent, etiamsi deinde sensu vel usum rationis amiserint, nihilominus absolute praebeatur.

The provisions of the Code in regard to baptism and extreme unction are repeated verbatim in the Roman Ritual.[10] In addition the Roman Ritual provides for the administration of the sacrament of penance to those who are destitute of their senses, on condition that they have expressed previously a desire for the sacrament.[11]

D. Theologians Teach That a Habitual Intention Is Sufficient

From official documents it has been shown that the Church has consistently recognized the sufficiency of a habitual intention, at least for the dying destitute of their senses, in the reception of baptism, extreme unction, penance, and the Eucharist. Nothing has been said about confirmation and holy orders. In regard to confirmation this silence may be explained by the fact that this sacrament is not one that is necessary for salvation, and hence was not commonly conferred even in the hour of death. Moreover, the ordinary minister of the sacrament was the bishop,

[10] *Rituale Romanum,* Pauli V Pontificis Maximi iussu editum aliorumque Pontificum cura recognitum atque auctoritate SSmi D. N. Pii Papae XI ad normam Codicis Iuris Canonici accommodatum (3. ed., New York, 1947), Tit. II, c. 3, n. 1; Tit. V, c. 1, n. 11.

[11] *Rituale Romanum,* Tit. III, c. 1, n. 25.

who often could only with difficulty be present at the time of the danger of death. In regard to holy orders, the sick destitute of their senses could not touch the instruments of ordination, an act which many up until recently regarded as constituting the matter of the sacrament.

The earlier writers indicated their own conviction of the sufficiency of a habitual intention when they spoke of the administration of the sacraments to the insane who had formerly enjoyed the use of reason. Thus St. Thomas wrote:

> With regard to these we must be guided by their wishes as expressed by them when sane. If, on the other hand, while sane they showed no desire to receive baptism, they must not be baptized.[12]

There might be others who had been insane from infancy, but who at times enjoyed lucid intervals during which they were able to reason more or less clearly. Since they did have periodic intervals during which they were capable of reasoning, they could not be classed as infants, and thus an intention was required. If such an intention, however, was present, they could be baptized even during their period of insanity. The proper procedure was to await one of their lucid intervals and then, upon their expression of a desire for it, to confer baptism, unless the danger of death intervened; even if this specific procedure was disregarded, however, the baptism, though illicit, was still to be regarded as valid.[13]

The principle in accordance with which the Decretalists judged the case was expressed thus:

> Voluntas semel habita et expressa, semper praesumitur durare.

[12] "Tales sunt judicandi secundum voluntatem quam habuerunt dum sanae mentis existerent. . . . Si nulla voluntas suscipiendi baptismum in eis apparuit dum sanae mentis essent, non sunt baptizandi."—St. Thomas, *Summa Theologica,* III, q. 68, a. 12.

[13] "Quidam vero sunt qui etsi a nativitate fuerint furiosi et amentes, habent tamen aliqua lucida intervalla, in quibus recta ratione uti possunt. Unde, si tunc baptizari voluerint, baptizari possunt etiam in amentia constituti. Et debet eis sacramentum tunc conferri si periculum timeatur: alioquin melius est ut tempus exspectetur in quo sint sanae mentis. . . ."—St. Thomas, *Summa Theologica,* III, q. 68, a. 12.

Thus, according to Hostiensis, if a person before he incurred insanity had the intention of being baptized, then the baptism would be validly conferred during his insanity; if his intention was to the contrary, i.e., if he cherished no wish for the reception of baptism, then the sacramental character would not be received.[14] Panormitanus also insisted that before they fell ill the insane had to have the intention to receive baptism, if later they were to receive the sacrament validly.[15] Boich (1310-1350) indicated that the minister needed to have some external signs of this previous intention, but that if these were indeed present the baptism was validly conferred.[16]

De Lugo believed that, once an understanding was gained of the different rôles played by the minister and the recipient in the conferring of the sacraments, then it became easier to comprehend why a virtual intention was demanded of the minister, whereas only a habitual intention was required of the recipient The minister needed to act as a true ministerial cause of the sacramental action. He needed to exert a real positive influence upon the act. For him the sacrament was, as Connell writes, a *"res facienda."* [17] Therefore, he had need of that kind of intention which would have such a positive influence upon the act. For this a habitual intention did not suffice, since by its very definition it no longer exercised any influence upon the act. Either a virtual or an actual intention was required.

On the other hand, for the reception of the sacraments it was simply required that the recipient render himself a fit subject, capable of receiving this gift from God. For him the sacrament

14 "Si ante erat in proposito baptizandi, character imprimitur et baptizatus est. Sin autem erat in voluntate contraria, scilicet non baptizandi, nullus character imprimitur."—Hostiensis, *Summa Aurea,* Lib. III, tit. 42, n. 10.

15 "Amentes vel dormientes baptizati, si ante dementiam vel dormitionem baptizari volebant, characterem suscipiunt; alias secus."—Panormitanus, Lib. III, tit. 42, c. 3, n. 1.

16 "Per certa signa vel alias qualitercumque de proposito baptizandi quia velit baptizare, et tunc si baptizetur, recepit characterem sacramenti."—Boich, *In Quinque Decretalium Libros Commentaria* (Venetiis, 1576), Lib. III, tit. 42, c. *non ut apponeres,* n. 4.

17 *De Sacramentis Ecclesiae,* n. 60.

was a gift, a "res recipienda." [18] For this there sufficed that kind of intention which simply sufficed for the acceptance of a gift, an intention once made but never revoked, even though it no longer had any influence on the act of acceptance.

The minister of the sacrament needed to function as the minister of Christ, in the name of Christ and of His Church. Therefore, at the time of the administration he had to act in a truly human manner; not so the recipient, who neither needed to be the cause of the sacrament, nor was required to receive the sacrament through any performance of a human act.[19]

It was, of course, required that at some time in the past the person had by means of a truly human act indicated a desire or an intention to receive the sacrament. Furthermore, it was necessary that he have never revoked this desire. Perhaps he had given no further thought to the reception of the sacrament; perhaps his earlier original intention did not exercise any actual influence in bringing him into a position in which he could receive the sacraments. As long as this previous intention had never been revoked, this person possessed a sufficient intention for the valid reception of the sacrament.[20] Though Vazquez treated directly of baptism, he did not limit this rule to that sacrament alone, for he readily acknowledged that the same principle was applicable in regard to the other sacraments as well.[21]

Sporer, too, in seeking to distinguish between the different requirements for an intention in the minister and in the recipient, laid stress on their distinctive functions in the conferring of the sacrament. The minister had to perform his rôle as a true cause of the sacramental act. The recipient, however, could be pas-

[18] Connell, *De Sacramentis Ecclesiae,* n. 60.

[19] De Lugo, *De Sacramentis in Genere,* Disp. ix, n. 132.

[20] "Ut quis verum recipiat sacramentum non opus est ad illud proxime aut remote ex tali voluntate moveri et accedere ita ut receptio illa sacramenti ex ea voluntate, remote saltem derivatur . . . sed sufficit prius consensisse, neque umquam contradixisse, etiamsi postea ipsi nihil de sacramento cogitanti nec ex illa voluntate ullo modo ad sacramentum accedenti baptismus conferatur."—Vazquez, *Commentarii,* Q. 69, a. 10, disp. 157, c. 2, n. 12.

[21] "Et idem . . . de quovis alio (sacramento) dicendum existimo."—*Commentarii,* Q. 69, a. 10, disp. 157, c. 2, n. 14.

sive; his previous consent, if it remained unrevoked, provided the requisite disposition essential for the reception of the sacrament and of the sacrament's effects.[22]

In support of the view that a habitual intention sufficed for the reception of the sacraments, St. Alphonsus pointed to the practice of the Church in his own time, which did not permit the repetition of the administration either of baptism or of holy orders as long as there was certainty that these sacraments had been received with a habitual intention.[23]

E. The Habitual Intention Is Sufficient for All the Sacraments

Today, all authors accept this conclusion that inherently (*per se*) a habitual intention suffices for all the sacraments, if considered from the viewpoint of the recipient.[24] It is true that a number of authors have taught that for penance and matrimony a virtual intention is required. These authors, however, have failed to distinguish adequately between the confection of the sacraments and their reception. In penance, for example, there is certainly required at least a virtual intention, if one considers the acts of the penitent which are necessary as the matter of this sacrament. However, if one considers only the absolution, through which there is truly actualized the reception of the sacrament, then there is no doubt that a habitual intention proved sufficient for a valid absolution. Certainly, no one questions the validity of the absolution of a dying man destitute of his senses.

F. Revocation of the Intention Must Flow from a Human Act

Thus it seems evident that a previous intention if never revoked could prove sufficient for a valid reception of the sacraments. However, just as the act by which the intention was

22 "Suscipiens sacramentum habet se passive tantum ideoque in eo non requiritur intentio quae sit causa actionis sacramentalis, sed solum quae sit dispositio ad suscipiendum sacramentum et recipiendum effectum sacramentalem."—*Theologia Moralis Sacramentalis,* Pars I, c. 2, sect. 3, n. 145.

23 *Theologia Moralis,* Lib. VI, n. 81.

24 Doronzo, *De Sacramentis in Genere* (Milwaukee: Bruce, 1946), p. 355; Connell, *De Sacramentis Ecclesiae,* n. 60; Cappello, *De Sacramentis,* I, n. 73.

first elicited had to be a truly human act, so too the revocation of the intention had to be a human act. Thus, if a person who had previously elicited an intention to receive a sacrament fell into insanity, he could during this insanity still receive that sacrament validly. What if he refused during his insanity to receive the sacrament? What if he resisted and fought against its administration? Under such circumstances the minister was simply to disregard the objections of the dying man, since his resistance could not be considered a revocation of his earlier intention. Such a revocation had to proceed from the person's intellect and will; it had to be a human act. In the case in question, however, the insane man was incapable of such a human act. Thus the habitual intention was not revoked, but under the circumstances was to be regarded as continuing, so that the insane man still remained a fit subject for the sacrament.[25]

The insane person perhaps with physical violence indicated an apparent reluctance regarding the reception of the sacrament. However, as long as a habitual intention continued to be present, the priest did not need to entertain any fears about the valid administration of the sacrament.[26] The physical opposition of an insane person, his repugnance, is neither free nor voluntary. Hence, in a moral question such as this it cannot prevent or hinder the validity of the sacrament.[27]

[25] "Haec revocatio non est actus humanus vel liber; ergo prior volitio humana et libera permanet habitualiter."—Lacroix, *Theologia Moralis,* Lib. VI, n. 176.

[26] "[Valide suscipit sacramentum] adultus maniacus aut phraeneticus qui manibus pedibusque repugnant volenti extreme se inungere; quia remanet nihilominus in eo habitualiter voluntas implicita suscipiendi hoc sacramentum quam habuit ante morbum."—Sporer, *Theologia Moralis Sacramentalis,* Pars I, c. 2, sect. 3, n. 143.

[27] "Si post adeptum usum rationis inciderunt in amentiam, adhuc sint capaces sacramentorum, si nihil aliud obstet quam amentis repugnantia, quae cum non sit voluntaria ac libera, in re morali nihil potest impedire."—Sporer, *Theologia Moralis Sacramentalis,* Pars I, c. 2, sect. 3, n. 143.

CHAPTER V

AN IMPLICIT INTENTION SUFFICES FOR THE RECEPTION OF THE SACRAMENTS

Up to this point it has been shown that for those who have reached the use of reason an intention is required if they are to receive the sacraments validly. There is one possible exception to this general rule, namely in regard to the Holy Eucharist. Furthermore, it has been demonstrated that neither an actual nor a virtual intention is required for the recipient of the sacrament. A habitual intention is sufficient. Such an intention, then, consists in an act of the will once made, never retracted, and which is not adverted to when the person receives the individual sacrament. The reception of the sacrament is an act which is done in accordance with the previous intention, though not because of that previous intention.

Turning from that aspect of the intention which considers it as an act of the will, it remains now to consider the intention in regard to its object, and more precisely in regard to the object as it is known, understood and willed by the person. The question to be answered here is whether the recipient must intend explicitly to receive the sacrament, i.e., to intend it as something clearly known and understood, or whether an implicit intention, i.e., to intend to receive it only insofar as it is contained and bound up in some other object which is explicitly willed, is sufficient.

A. An Implicit Intention Suffices for Baptism

1. An Explicit Intention Is Usually Present

An adult is to be baptized only after he has completed a course of instruction in the Catholic faith.[1] The amount of instruction which precedes baptism will of course vary according to the individual case. A summary of the minimum instruction

[1] "Adultus, nisi sciens et volens probeque instructus, ne baptizetur."—canon **752, § 1.**

required has been given by the Congregation for the Propagation of the Faith. This summary includes those doctrines which theologians commonly propose as being either essentially (*de necessitate medii*) or also preceptively (*de necessitate praecepti*) necessary.[2] The kind of instruction will also vary according to the individual. It too will be adapted to his needs and his capabilities.[3]

These provisions of canon 752, § 1, are applicable only in the ordinary situation wherein one is dealing with normal healthy adults. If, however, the person is in danger of death, then in the presence of this new circumstance the law makes different provisions. If the person, though in danger of death, nevertheless retains the use of his senses, then some sort of religious instruction is still to be given. Frequently, because of the weakened condition of the person, this instruction will be limited to the principal mysteries of the Catholic faith.[4] However, the condition of the dying person may be such so as not to permit even this rudimentary instruction. In this case it will be enough if the person in some way manifests his assent to these great religious truths and his willingness to live a Christian life.[5]

In its first two paragraphs, then, canon 752 has made provision for three distinct situations which may confront the minister of baptism. The first case is that of a normal, healthy adult; the second, of an adult in danger of death, but still capable of some instruction in the faith; the third case is that of an adult also in danger of death, able only to give external assent to the faith, but incapable of further instruction. In all three cases, however,

[2] S. C. de Prop. Fide, instr. (ad Vic. Ap. Sin.), 18 oct. 1883, ad XVII: "Quapropter Sacra Congregatio . . . statuit, ut cum agitur de ordinariis casibus conversionis adultorum, et excepto mortis eorum periculo, haec pro oculis a missionariis habeantur, antequam eos ad baptismum admittant, nempe ut catechumeni cognoscant principalia mysteria fidei, Symbolum, Orationem dominicam, decalogum, praecepta Ecclesiae, effectum baptismi, actus virtutum theologalium earumque motiva."—*Fontes,* n. 4903.

[3] Waldron, *The Minister of Baptism,* The Catholic University of America Canon Law Studies, n. 170 (Washington, D. C.: The Catholic University of America Press, 1942), p. 89, note 63.

[4] Canon 752, § 2.

[5] Canon 752, § 2.

some knowledge of the faith is possessed. In the light of a previous instruction and in consequence of the knowledge thus possessed, the person will be able to receive the sacrament while he is conscious and thus knowingly entertains an explicit intention to receive baptism.

2. The Desire to Become a Christian Contains a Sufficient Implicit Intention

Canon 752, § 3, deals with a fourth possible situation which the minister of baptism may meet. The subject of the sacrament who is in danger of death may also be destitute of his senses. Manifestly, he is unable now to make a formal request to receive baptism. In such a case the Code provides that, if the person has at any time manifested in some probable fashion an intention to receive baptism, then the minister of the sacrament is obliged to confer baptism on him at least conditionally.[6]

It remains, then, for theologians and canonists to indicate the extent of the meaning of the phrase *"aliquo probabili modo."* There can be no question, of course, that an explicit request to receive baptism, if made earlier when the person was still in possession of his senses, would fall under the scope of this canon. In fact, one can say with equal certainty that even an implicit intention contained in the simple fact of a previous acceptance of Christianity would be sufficient, even though the person has never heard specifically of baptism and of its necessity.

> Valeret baptismus, si aliquis religionem Christianam corde amplexus esset, licet nihil de baptismo aut eius necessitate audisset; hic enim licet morbo oppressus, sensibus destitueretur, baptizaretur valide, quia voluit absolute hanc religionem amplecti, eiusque ritibus, quicumque illi essent, gubernari.[7]

Sporer cited as an example of this a catechumen who while in danger of death has remained ignorant of the very existence of baptism as a sacramental means of salvation. He too believed

[6] "Quod si baptismum ne petere quidem queat, sed vel antea vel in praesenti statu manifestaverit aliquo probabili modo intentionem illum suscipiendi, baptizandus est sub conditione."—canon 752, § 3.

[7] De Lugo, *De Sacramentis in Genere,* Disp. ix, n. 130.

that there can be no question as to the validity of the sacrament, because he felt that the wish to receive baptism is implicitly contained in the desire to embrace Christianity.[8] For this reason, then, Vermeersch strongly supported the opinion that regards the implicit intention contained in the desire to accept the Christian religion as sufficient for the valid reception of baptism, and he pointed to it as a conclusion accepted by all authors as certain.

> Nemo enim negarit valere baptismum collatum alicui moribundo qui explicite voluerit fieri christianus, sed de ipso baptismo nullam habuerit notitiam.[9]

3. Supernatural Attrition Probably Contains a Sufficient Implicit Intention

Is this the farthest extent of a sufficient implicit intention? An imposing list of authors contends that it is not. A number of writers, both early and modern, believe that anyone who has a true supernatural attrition for his sins has at the same time a sufficient intention for the reception of a valid baptism, at least when he is in danger of death and destitute of his senses.

True sorrow for sin includes, so they state, the will to do all that is necessary for salvation and to observe all the commandments that indicate what is necessary for salvation. Now, all men have an obligation to enter the true Church. This they will do through the reception of baptism, which is the doorway to the Church. Therefore, there is contained in true sorrow for sin the further desire to enter Christ's Church and to receive baptism. Thus, in all those who have at least attrition, there is to be found an implicit desire for baptism as well.

> Quicumque vult fieri christianus, atque adeo omnis qui habet veram contritionem de peccatis censetur implicite petere baptismum, etsi de eo nihil umquam audiverit, quia talis dolor includit virtuale propositum servandi omnia praecepta ad talem finem necessaria quorum unum est praeceptum suscipiendi baptismum.[10]

[8] *Theologia Moralis Sacramentalis,* Pars I, c. 2, sect. 3, n. 149.

[9] Vermeersch, "Practica disquisitio de sacramentis conferendis vel negandis acatholico," *Periodica,* XVIII (1929), 129*.

[10] DeConinck, as cited by Vermeersch, *loc. cit.*

Lacroix wrote in a very similar vein:

> Sufficit implicita [intentio] tantum, contenta in contritione vel attritione . . . quia in hac includitur votum servandi omnia praecepta, item accipiendi omnia media necessaria ad salutem, adeoque etiam suscipiendi baptismum.[11]

It is interesting to note that Sporer extended this doctrine so far as to apply it to the case of a dying Jew, provided he had attrition for his sins. Undoubtedly, Sporer made use of this example because he believed that the possibility of an implicit intention to embrace Christianity and to receive baptism would be the most remote in a Jew. Thus, by this example, he indicated the applicability of this doctrine to all cases wherein there was present a true supernatural attrition.[12] Sporer, in fact, believed that such a baptism would not only be valid, but also licit, despite the fact that the Jew had earlier resisted all efforts to convert him and had even stated that he preferred death to baptism.[13]

The defense of this view was taken up in recent times by Vermeersch, who started with the basic premise: *sacramenta propter homines*. Therefore, he argued, the administration of the sacraments is always to be regarded as licit until the prohibition thereof can be clearly demonstrated. He rejected the argument which is based upon the reverence due to the sacraments, since he felt that this demand is satisfactorily met through their conditional administration. Moreover, he believed that it is not necessary that there be present some well-founded probability for the validity of the sacrament to be conferred. The need for any degree of certainty as to the effect is excluded, so he contended, by the extreme necessity that attends the case. When a man is dying, it is only reasonable that we should make use not only of

[11] *Theologia Moralis,* Lib. VI, n. 168.

[12] "Judaeus qui habet veram attritionem supernaturalem de peccatis . . . licite baptizatur in extremo agone constitutus, ratione ac sensibus destitutus quia in tali attritione etiam implicite involvitur voluntas servandi omnia praecepta (adeoque etiam baptismum suscipiendi) ad salutem aeternam consequendam necessaria."—Sporer, *Theologia Moralis Sacramentalis,* Pars I, c. 2, sect. 3, n. 151.

[13] *Loc. cit.*

certain and even probably efficacious remedies, but also of any such means which have not been shown to be wholly useless. Hence, Vermeersch believed that the sacrament can be administered whenever there is no certainty of its invalidity, in the absence, of course, of any positive prohibition on the part of the Church.[14]

Other equally eminent authors insisted that no one should be required to undertake the grave obligations of membership in the Church without knowing at least in a confused way what it is that he is entering. Hence they believed that for baptism a more express intention is required than for some of the other sacraments. Suarez wrote:

> Hunc consensum quem necesse est praecessisse, quando actu non adest, non esse eodem modo necessarium in omnibus sacramentis. Baptismus, quia est ianua ad Ecclesiam et in eo fit prima solemnis professio fidei et legis Christi, ideo videtur requirere in adulto voluntatem magis expressam et formalem.[15]

The basis for the distinction between baptism and the other sacraments is to be found, first of all, in the fact that with the other sacraments the duties and demands involved exist in smaller measure. Thus the presence of an intention can be more easily presumed.

> Dicta sacramenta minus incommodi vel oneris afferunt secum; ergo facilius praesumitur volitio generalis habendi talia bona.[16]

Moreover, as has been seen in the quotation from Suarez, baptism is the doorway and the entrance to the Church. At the moment of baptism there takes place the solemn acceptance of the moral and doctrinal teaching of the Church and its founder, Jesus Christ. Hence, it seems reasonable that one would expect a more explicit intention to be demanded for this most important sacrament of initiation.

[14] *Ibid.*, p. 127*.

[15] *Commentarius,* Q. 64, a. 10, disp. xiv, sect. 2.

[16] Lacroix, *Theologia Moralis,* Lib. VI, n. 172.

Again, such sacraments as the Holy Eucharist and extreme unction are received by those who wish to live and die in the Catholic faith. They wish to be ruled as other Catholics; they wish to receive the sacraments which other Catholics receive when they are ill. Included in this desire, then, is an intention sufficient for the reception of these sacraments.

One who is a Jew, however, wishes to live and die in the Jewish faith. He wishes to be ruled by its laws; he wishes to make use of its religious practices and rites. He too has the desire to observe all of God's commands. Therefore, if baptism is something which God commands him to receive, he has an implicit desire to receive it. However, he falls under such an obligation only after he has examined the truth of the Gospel and has acknowledged it to be true. Only then does his obligation begin, only then is he bound to receive baptism, only then will the implicit intention that is contained in the intention to observe all of God's laws be sufficiently determined.[17]

It appears, then, that the implicit intention that is contained in supernatural attrition is not sufficient for a valid reception of baptism. However, because of the number and the authority of the authors who hold the contrary view, the sufficiency of such an intention cannot be denied at least extrinsic probability. Hence, in a case of necessity, if no other avenue is available, it seems an acceptable practice to utilize this opinion in one's efforts to assist the dying person in whatever rightful manner assistance may be given. This, for example, is the conclusion of King, who wrote:

> Thus, it would seem . . . that the affirmative opinion has but slight intrinsic foundation from the viewpoint of intention, although it has sufficient extrinsic probability for the conditional administration of Baptism in the hypothesis.[18]

Cappello arrived at a similar conclusion, but indicated that in

[17] Merkelbach, *Summa Theologiae Moralis,* III, 93; De Lugo, *De Sacramentis in Genere,* disp. ix, n. 130.

[18] King, *The Administration of the Sacraments to Dying Non-Catholics,* The Catholic University of America Canon Law Studies, n. 23 (Washington, D. C.: The Catholic University of America, 1924), p. 15.

his own mind there was an obligation on the part of the minister of the sacraments to avail himself of this opinion in favor of the dying man.

> Proinde in casu necessitatis, si aliter fieri nequeat, potes ac debes eiusmodi opinione uti ad vitam aeternam moribundi sensibus destituti, quantum in te est, procurandam.[19]

B. An Implicit Intention Suffices for Confirmation

1. An Explicit Intention Is Usually Present

In the sacramental economy of the Church there exists a very close link between the sacraments of baptism and confirmation. In the ancient Church and up until the XII century confirmation was conferred immediately after baptism. Present-day legislation has altered this practice, however, so that confirmation now is regularly deferred until the seventh year or even later.[20] Commonly, a period of instruction precedes the reception of this sacrament.[21] This instruction will usually include a knowledge of the rudiments of the faith as well as "an understanding of the meaning and of the effects of confirmation." [22] As a result of this previous instruction the recipient should be enabled under ordinary circumstances to elicit an explicit intention in receiving the sacrament.

2. An Implicit Intention Is Sufficient

At other times, though, the recipient may be seriously ill, perhaps even unconscious, and thus unable to give any evidence of the presence of an intention. It may be impossible to ascertain whether he has ever in the past expressed an explicit desire to receive confirmation.

In 1946 the decree of the Sacred Congregation of the Sacraments, *Spiritus Sancti munera,* granted broad powers to pastors

[19] *De Sacramentis,* I, n. 150.

[20] Canon 788.

[21] Canon 786.

[22] Bennington, *The Subject of Confirmation,* The Catholic University of America Canon Law Studies, n. 267 (Washington, D. C.: The Catholic University of America Press, 1952), p. 104.

and to others to confer confirmation on those who are in danger of death due to a serious illness.[23] Hence, it is of even greater moment now to ascertain what kind of intention will suffice for a valid reception of confirmation and how its presence can be determined.

All authors agree that an explicit intention is not required for confirmation, at least not in the extreme cases of serious need, but that an implicit intention will suffice.[24]

3. A Catholic Life Contains Implicitly a Sufficient Intention

In seeking to determine whether an intention actually exists, "it may be possible to deduce from what is known of the person's ordinary manner of living the existence of a habitual intention on his part to receive confirmation."[25] Thus, if the pastor recognized the unconscious man as a very devout, practicing Catholic, he would not hesitate in affirming the presence of a habitual intention to receive confirmation. However, even this would not be required to provide certainty as to the presence of an intention. It would be enough for the minister to know that the unconscious man is a Catholic. Under such circumstances the Church presumes that when a person has freely chosen to become a member of Christ's Church through the reception of baptism, or when he has freely chosen to persevere in that membership, then there is implicitly contained in this the further desire and determination to receive the completion and the fulfillment of baptism, which is confirmation.

> Quilibet homo qui voluit fieri membrum verae ecclesiae per baptismum vel qui libere in illo statu permanet, eo ipso vult etiam huius status quasi naturale complementum. Complementum autem quoddam baptismi confirmatio est qua baptizatus quasi in adulta aetate vitae supernaturalis et Christianae constituitur.[26]

In addition every Catholic must be presumed to have the con-

[23] *AAS,* XXXVIII (1946), 349.

[24] Cappello, *De Sacramentis,* I, n. 74 (2).

[25] Bennington, *The Subject of Confirmation,* p. 100.

[26] Lehmkuhl, *Theologia Moralis,* II (9. ed., Friburgi Brisgoviae, 1898), n. 48.

stant desire to live and die as do other Catholics. Included in this desire will always be the intention of being fortified with the sacramental aids when they are required. Certainly, there can be no greater need for the sacraments than at the time of death. Hence, this general intention to receive the sacraments when needed most certainly includes the reception of the sacraments at that most crucial period. In reaching a decision the minister cannot hesitate, for the danger of death rules out the possibility of any postponement.[27]

The presumption of the presence of such an intention is further bolstered by the fact that this sacrament brings with it great spiritual advantages, while at the same time it does not entail any serious disadvantages.

This habitual implicit intention may find expression either in the form of a desire to receive the Church's sacraments at the moment of death, or, more generally, simply in the intention of making use of all those helps which are necessary or useful for salvation.

> Voluntas habitualis implicita in hoc sita est quod quis intentionem habuerit generalem et non retractavit, adhibendi ea quae saluti sint necessaria et utilia, vel in catholica religione vivendi et moriendi cum eiusdem religionis praesidiis; vel, a fortiori, omnia sacramenta in vita et morte recipiendi.[28]

Even the presence of serious sin in persons does not rule out the possibility of the simultaneous presence of a sincere, though inefficacious, desire to employ the sacraments of the Church as means of salvation for their souls. This is most especially true, if, despite their past delinquencies, they have remained attached to the Church.[29] Only when they have shown most clearly and most certainly their contumacious impenitence down to the very end should the sacrament be denied them.[30]

[27] Bennington, *The Subject of Confirmation,* p. 68.

[28] Bucceroni, *Institutiones Theologiae Moralis,* Vol. III (6. ed., Romae, 1915), n. 384.

[29] Noldin, *Summa Theologiae Moralis,* III, n. 41 (5a).

[30] ". . . constet eos usque ad deliquium manifeste impoenitentes fuisse."—Noldin, *Summa Theologiae Moralis,* III, n. 41 (5a).

C. An Implicit Intention Suffices for the Eucharist

1. *For the Eucharist as Viaticum an Implicit Intention Is Sufficient*

The Eucharist, in addition to being the Daily Bread with which the Christian life is nourished, serves also as a remedy for the dying. In the form of Holy Viaticum it provides the aid and the strength to enable the dying to persevere in grace and to remain steadfast in their faith.

On the basis of this twofold rôle which the Eucharist plays in the sacramental life of every Catholic, authors frequently distinguish between the case wherein the Eucharist is to be received in the form of Viaticum and the case wherein it is received under its more frequent form of daily spiritual refreshment.

All authors agree that when the Eucharist is administered in the form of Viaticum to those who are in danger of death, then only a minimal form of intention will be required. At such a time, then, an implicit habitual intention will be sufficient for a valid and fruitful reception of that sacrament.[31] In support of his view, De Lugo cited the practice prevalent in his own time, in accordance with which the Church granted the Eucharist to those who had been seized with a sudden illness in which they became deprived of the use of their senses.[32] De Lugo allowed the same practice to be observed in regard to the insane when they were in danger of death, provided that they had enjoyed the use of reason previously in their lives, and provided that it could be legitimately presumed that at the time they were in the state of grace.[33]

Noldin also allowed the administration of the Eucharist in the form of Viaticum to those who were destitute of their senses, provided that they had at least a habitual intention, and as long as proper care was taken for the avoidance of all danger of irreverence toward the sacrament.[34] Thus it has been the practice

[31] De Lugo, *De Sacramentis in Genere,* disp. ix, n. 126; Lacroix, *Theologia Moralis,* Lib. VI, n. 170; Merkelbach, *Summa Theologiae Moralis,* III, n. 270; Cappello, *De Sacramentis,* I, n. 74.

[32] *De Sacramentis in Genere,* Disp. ix, n. 126.

[33] *Loc. cit.*

[34] *Summa Theologiae Moralis,* III, n. 135.

of the Church up until the present time to grant the Eucharist as Viaticum even in those cases wherein at most only an implicit habitual intention was present. This the Church could not have allowed unless at the same time it had acknowledged the sufficiency of this intention for a valid and fruitful reception of the sacrament.

2. The Desire to Live and Die as a Catholic Contains a Sufficient Intention

This implicit habitual intention is contained in a Catholic's desire to live and die as a Catholic. Contained in that general intention is the more specific intention to receive the sacraments which the Church confers at the time and in the manner in which they are to be received. Now, the Church has a long-established practice of administering certain sacraments, namely penance, extreme unction, and Holy Viaticum, to the dying. Hence, contained in that first very general intention—implicitly of course—is the intention to receive Holy Viaticum at the moment when one's life is ebbing away.

The Church always assumes that this intention is actually present in all who have lived Catholic lives. Therefore, as long as there is no serious danger of irreverence to the sacrament, the Church wishes these sacraments to be administered, even when no explicit request has been previously made for them.[35]

In cases of doubt the presumption is always to be made in favor of the dying person. Thus, as long as there is no certainty that he has remained contumaciously impenitent, and as long as he has retained his communion with the Church, it can rightfully be presumed that such a Catholic has the sufficient desire to receive the sacrament.

> Ergo cum in extremis etiam solum dubium sufficiat, quilibet Catholicus quem non constat mansisse in impietate vel qui mansit in unione Ecclesiae iure censetur eam intentionem habuisse quae requiritur et sufficit ut extrema unctio et Viaticum voluntarie suscipi dicantur.[36]

The sacrament then is to be denied only when there is danger of irreverence, when there is unassailable certainty of the pres-

[35] Sporer, *Theologia Moralis Sacramentalis,* Pars I, c. 2, sect. 3, n. 154.

[36] Lehmkuhl, *Theologia Moralis,* II, n. 48.

ence of the guilt of serious sin, or when there is hope for a sufficient recovery to allow the sacrament to be conferred while he is in possession of his senses.

3. Outside of Viaticum Many Authors Require an Explicit Habitual Intention

Though they are in agreement in acknowledging the sufficiency of an implicit habitual intention for the Eucharist when It is administered to the dying in the form of Viaticum, the authors do not display the same unanimity in doctrine when discussing the further question of the nature of the recipient's intention for the reception of the Eucharist in a form other than that of Holy Viaticum. As Statkus writes: "Outside the danger of death an explicit intention of receiving the Eucharist is demanded, but an implicit intention suffices when the danger of death is present." [37] Numerous other authors have made the same distinction, requiring at least an explicit habitual intention for the reception of the Eucharist outside of those cases wherein It is administered in the form of Viaticum.[38]

The very *res-sacramentum* of the Eucharist consists in the presence of Christ as a guest in the soul. This sacramental presence of Christ as a guest is effected through an act of the will on the part of the recipient; more specifically, it is by his intention that the Eucharistic species is voluntarily consumed, so that Christ is made present as the guest of the soul. Thus, if a consecrated host were eaten by a dog, Christ would not be *sacramentally* present to the dog, since there would be lacking the requirement of a voluntary reception.[39] The only exceptions to

[37] *The Minister of the Last Sacraments,* The Catholic University of America Canon Law Studies, n. 299 (Washington, D. C.: The Catholic University of America Press, 1951), p. 121.

[38] "Ad Eucharistiam requiritur saltem habitualis intentio, attamen in moribundo etiam interpretativam sufficere. . . ."—Lacroix, *Theologia Moralis,* Lib. VI, n. 170; De Lugo, *De Sacramentis in Genere,* Disp. ix. n. 127; Noldin, *Summa Theologiae Moralis,* III, n. 133; Vermeersch, *Theologia Moralis,* III, n. 185; Pruemmer, *Manuale Theologiae Moralis,* III, n. 87; Lehmkuhl, *Theologia Moralis,* II, n. 48.

[39] Umberg, "De Reviviscentia Sacramentorum Ratione Rei et Sacramenti," *Periodica,* XVII (1928), 22*-23*; Noldin, *Summa Theologiae Moralis,* III, n. 133.

this requirement according to Noldin are infants and those to whom the Eucharist is given in the form of Viaticum, for their intention, i.e., infants', is provided by Christ and by the Church.[40]

St. Thomas considered the case of one who consumes a consecrated host which he does not know to be consecrated. He likened this situation to the one in which an animal has eaten a consecrated host. In neither case can one speak of a sacramental consuming of the Body of Christ.

> Unde non sacramentaliter, sed per accidens corpus Christi manducat: sicut manducaret ille qui sumeret hostiam consecratam quia nesciens eam esse consecratam.[41]

Numerous authors, down through the centuries from the time of St. Thomas, have considered this same problem, namely, what must be said of the validity of the sacrament when a person consumes a host without knowing that it is consecrated. Many authors agree with St. Thomas that to receive the Eucharist under such circumstances would not be to receive it in a sacramental fashion. They insist that for a truly sacramental reception of the Eucharist an intention is required.

> Si quis casu comederet hostiam consecratam putans esse panem alium, non fore sumptionem sacramentalem, nec ideo recipiat gratiam, nam nullam videtur habere intentionem sumendi nisi sumat more Catholico. . . . Consequenter non voluit sumere . . . quando putaret se profanum panem sumere. . . .[42]

Without an intention, however, there would be a purely material reception of the Eucharist, and thus no grace would be conferred.

[40] "Debent autem excipere casum viatici et infantes baptizatos in quibus intentio illa habetur per Christum vel ecclesiam."—Noldin, *Summa Theologiae Moralis,* III, n. 133; "In infantibus, Christi eucharistica praesentia, etiam absque ipsorum intentione Christum excipiendi, potest esse vere hospitalis, quia ad eos Ipse se invitat, ut dici solet, si quando aliquis princeps tamquam hospes apud aliquem inferiorem vult divertere."—Umberg, *loc. cit.*

[41] *Summa Theologica,* q. 80, a. 3, ad 3.

[42] Lacroix, *Theologia Moralis,* Lib. VI, n. 178.

> . . . qui sumeret hostiam quam consecratam esse nescit, sumeret quidem verum corpus Christi, sed materialiter tantum et sine fructu, si omnis intentio defuisset.[43]

Such a reception of the Eucharist might be considered on a par with that when the Eucharist is received by an unbaptized person.

> Qui ergo inveniret hostiam et putans non esse consecratam eam sumeret, secundum hanc sententiam mere materialiter susciperet Eucharistiam, sicut non baptizatus.[44]

Vazquez sought for the reason why such a reception would not be a sacramental one. He believed that the reason was to be found in the well-founded presumption that the recipient would not want to consume the Eucharist under such irreverent circumstances. Moreover, he argued, the subject already had the simple intention to eat what he erroneously thought to be ordinary bread. Therefore, with this intention already present, there was precluded the further intention of eating this bread as the Bread of Angels.[45]

De Lugo did not accept this line of argumentation. He rather preferred to point out that a Catholic's general intention of receiving the sacraments, which allows the administering of Viaticum to a person destitute of his senses though he has never expressly requested It, does not ordinarily extend beyond their reception when he is in danger of death. He acknowledged that a Catholic could indeed include in his general intention of receiving the sacraments the further specific intention of receiving the Eucharist even outside the time of danger of death. However, he denied that this intention, granted its presence, would include even those times when the recipient believes that he is eating only ordinary bread. Therefore, De Lugo concluded, since this reception of the Eucharist is neither voluntary nor willed, it does not cause or produce the sacramental effect.[46]

[43] Pruemmer, *Manuale Theologiae Moralis,* III, n. 87.

[44] Noldin, *Summa Theologiae Moralis,* III, n. 133.

[45] *Commentarii,* Q. 80, a. 9, disp. 212, c. 2, n. 7.

[46] *De Sacramentis in Genere,* Disp. ix, n. 127.

4. Other Authors Admit an Implicit Habitual Intention Suffices in All Cases

Bucceroni took up De Lugo's suggestion that the general intention could suffice for a sacramental reception of the Eucharist at other times than when the recipient is in danger of death, and then sought to determine at which times that might be. He concluded that such a general intention could also be sufficient for a sacramental reception whenever the reception of the Eucharist was a matter of serious obligation. Moreover, so he argued, if the desire to die in a Catholic manner contained implicitly the intention to receive the sacraments which the Church gives to the dying, including Viaticum, why was it not equally true to say that in the desire to live a Catholic life there was contained a sufficient desire to receive this sacrament during life? Thus, from the very existence of the desire to make use of all the means established by divine decree as useful or necessary for salvation, he believed that there derived a sufficient intention for even a devotional reception of the Eucharist in a sacramental manner.[47]

Other authors, however, deny that any intention is required for a valid reception of the Eucharist.[48] As a sacrament the Eucharist is unique. It alone of all the sacraments exists sacramentally before its sacramental use. Baptism does not exist apart from its matter and form and the intentions of its minister and its recipient; the same is true of the other sacraments as well. However, the Eucharist does not depend on any human subject for its existence. It does not require any previous disposition on his part to exist as a sacrament.[49]

Hence, so Cappello argues, since the Eucharist is a permanent sacrament, existing independently of any subjective dispositions, this sacrament is never received invalidly by a baptized person, but only unfruitfully. Cappello considers this view, so strongly espoused by him, to be "true and certain."[50] Connell mentions

[47] *Institutiones Theologiae Moralis,* III, p. 248.

[48] *Iorio, Theologia Moralis,* III, n. 35 (7); Cappello, *De Sacramentis,* I, n. 74.

[49] Sporer, *Theologia Moralis Sacramentalis,* Pars I, c. 2, sect. 3, n. 144.

[50] *De Sacramentis,* I, n. 74.

authors who, with reference to a person who unknowingly and unwittingly swallows a consecrated host, deem his reception not only a valid but also a fruitful one, provided that the person is baptized and is properly disposed.[51]

In this view, then, the distinction between the intention as required for Viaticum and as required for a Communion of devotion would be one that looks rather to a licit than to the valid reception of the sacrament.[52]

D. An Implicit Intention Suffices for Penance

The sacrament of penance differs from the other sacraments in so far as it is in its essential nature a judgment. The rôle of the priest-confessor is that of a judge who hears the cases and passes sentence. The penitent is both the accuser and the accused. It is he who ordinarily presents the case for a decision; the judge does not begin the case on his own initiative. Therefore, whenever the penitent is able, he must make an explicit accusation of his own guilt; if this is not possible, then he should at least request the intervention of the judge by manifesting in some way a desire to confess.[53]

The III Council of Carthage (397) permitted the administration of the sacrament of penance to the sick destitute of their senses, if there were present others who could testify that the dying man had previously requested the sacrament.[54]

Similar provisions are to be found in the IV Council of Carthage (398),[55] and the I Council of Orange(441).[56] The present Roman Ritual allows for the absolution of a dying person who

[51] "Nonnulli ab hac regula de necessitate intentionis ex parte subjecti excipiunt Eucharistiam, dicentes (probabiliter saltem) hoc sacramentum valide—et, si nullus ponatur obex, etiam fructuose—suscipi a baptizato, qui inadvertenter hostiam consecratam deglutit."—*De Sacramentis Ecclesiae*, n. 59.

[52] Cappello, *De Sacramentis*, I, n. 74.

[53] De Lugo, *De Sacramentis in Genere*, Disp. ix, n. 124.

[54] C. 75, D. IV, *de cons.*

[55] C. 8, C. XXVI, q. 6.

[56] C. 7, C. XXVI, q. 6.

has either personally or through others indicated a desire to confess.[57]

According to many writers this desire to confess must be externally manifested. An internal act of the will alone is not regarded by them as sufficient, since this sacrament is an external judgment in which both the accusation of the sins and the consequent sentence must be truly perceptible by the senses.[58] Thus De Lugo, Suarez, Laymann and others insist that before absolution can be given to a dying person destitute of his senses there must be proof of his earlier desire for the sacrament, such as is required in the early conciliar legislation. When such testimony of an earlier desire is wanting, then absolution must be denied under the circumstances.

These writers base their view upon the commonly accepted theological opinion that the acts of the penitent, namely, confession, contrition, and satisfaction constitute the matter of the sacrament. Therefore, for the sacrament they must be perceptible by the senses.

Other authors, like Sporer, Lacroix, St. Alphonsus, and most of the moderns, believe that, despite the absence of testimony regarding a previous request for the sacrament, nevertheless the dying man can be licitly absolved.[59]

These authors did not reject the doctrine of the other authors, which regarded the acts of the penitent as the matter of the sacrament, but they believed that in the Catholic life of the penitent there is to be found a reasonable basis for the assumption that at some time previously he has expressed at least implicitly such a desire for the sacrament and the requisite sorrow for his sins.[60]

Every Catholic is presumed to have the general desire to live and die as a Catholic. Included in this general desire, then, is the further wish to receive, and to be fortified by, those sacraments which the Church bestows upon her dying children, and

[57] *Rituale Romanum,* Tit. III, c. 1, n. 25.

[58] De Lugo, *De Sacramentis in Genere,* Disp. ix, n. 124.

[59] St. Alphonsus, *Theologia Moralis,* Lib. VI, n. 482; Cappello, *De Sacramentis,* II, n. 188.

[60] St. Alphonsus, *Theologia Moralis,* Lib. VI, n. 483.

included in a prominent place among these is surely the sacrament of penance. Therefore, every Catholic is presumed to have the further desire to be absolved in the danger of death. Pruemmer believed that the same intention can be found even among material heretics and schismatics.[61] Cappello, following the lead of St. Alphonsus, believes that such an intention can be presumed present even in those whose lives have been little influenced by their Catholic faith, and even in those who perhaps have been stricken and deprived of their senses in the very act of committing a serious sin.[62]

If contrition and confession are regarded as the matter of the sacrament, then they must be given external manifestation. This will be necessary for a valid absolution. Bonacina (ca. 1585-1631), Busenbaum (1600-1668) and Concina (1687-1756) held that the sorrow for sin must be elicited with the intention to confess the sin.[63] They argued that just as the minister of the sacrament must by his intention direct and determine the matter toward the confection of the sacrament and toward no other end, so too must the recipient of penance. Thus the sorrow for sins which is the matter of the sacrament must be always elicited with the intention to confess these sins.

Since this requirement is not listed by the Council of Trent in its enumeration of the qualities which are required for sufficient contrition, authorities commonly deny that such an intention is demanded.[64]

Authors, then, generally, conclude with Lacroix that an implicit habitual intention will suffice for a valid reception of the sacrament, provided that the penitent has in some way given external expression to his sorrow for sin and his confession thereof.

> Ad penitentiam requiritur saltem habitualis et sufficeret implicita vel interpretativa, dummodo dolorem aliquo signo

[61] Pruemmer, *Manuale Theologiae Moralis,* III, n. 326.

[62] Cappello, *De Sacramentis,* II, n. 188, 189.

[63] Cf. St. Alphonsus, *Theologia Moralis,* Lib. VI, n. 447.

[64] Cappello, *De Sacramentis,* II, n. 117, who cites for his view: De Lugo, Suarez, Ballerini-Palmieri.

> externo expressisset, quod signum esset loco confessionis seu accusationis sui.[65]

E. An Implicit Intention Suffices for Extreme Unction

1. The Code Teaches That an Implicit Intention Is Sufficient

Both the Code of Canon Law and the Roman Ritual indicate that an explicit intention is not demanded for the valid reception of extreme unction, but that an implicit intention is all that is required.

> Infirmis autem qui, cum suae mentis compotes essent, illud saltem implicite petierunt aut verisimiliter petiissent, etiamsi deinde sensus vel usum rationis amiserint, nihilominus absolute praebeatur.[66]

Canon 943 contemplates the situation wherein the sick person has lost the use of his senses. Thus he is no longer capable either of an actual or of a virtual intention; he is capable of no more than a habitual intention. However, the canon does not deal directly with the question of the presence of an intention; rather, it deals with the external manifestation of the intention, which itself is something internal.[67] It takes note of a request for the sacrament which has been made at some earlier time. Such a request for the sacrament obviously implies the presence of an intention to receive the sacrament, an intention which motivated the request. Canon 1086, § 1, states that the "internal consent of the mind is always presumed to be in conformity with the words or signs used in the contracting of a marriage." *A pari* the same presumption holds true in regard to the reception of the other sacraments as well. Now, such a request made in the past is deemed sufficient to allow the minister to confer the sacrament without condition. Evidently, then, the intention which lies behind the request is also to be regarded as sufficient to insure the validity of the sacrament.[68]

[65] Lacroix, *Theologia Moralis,* Lib. VI, n. 171.

[66] Canon 943; *Rituale Romanum,* Tit. V, c. 1, n. 11.

[67] Kilker, *Extreme Unction,* p. 252; Coronata, *De Sacramentis,* I (2. ed., Taurini: Marietti, 1951), p. 603, note 1.

[68] Kilker, *Extreme Unction,* p. 255.

The intention which is judged to be sufficient for the sacrament cannot be either an actual or even a virtual intention, since the sick man is bereft of his senses and incapable of eliciting either of these. Therefore, it is a habitual intention which the Code here deems sufficient for the reception of extreme unction.

Canon 943 further declares that the request for extreme unction can be made in either of two ways, either explicitly or implicitly. From the wording of the law it may seem that an explicit request is to be preferred, inasmuch as the request is to be made *saltem implicite.* In former times greater insistence was laid on such a formal request for the sake of a more literal compliance with the requirements stated in the Epistle of St. James: "Inducat presbyteros Ecclesiae. . . ." Kilker cites a number of old statutes and rituals which prescribed that the sick man must have specifically requested the sacrament before it was to be conferred.[69] Moreover, perhaps in this way it was also felt that the presence of a sufficient intention would be more adequately revealed.

Such an explicit intention for the sacrament is had when the person has previously made an actual request to have extreme unction administered to him when and if he should fall victim to a serious illness.

Canon 943, however, readily acknowledges that an explicit request for the sacrament is not always demanded. An implicit request will suffice (*saltem implicite*). In this regard Suarez had earlier written:

> [Sufficit ut] antequam aliquis amittat usum rationis, hoc sacramentum petierit aut si meminisset, petiturus fuisset. Et in hoc sensu dicunt fere Doctores omnes, quod licet ad recipiendum hoc sacramentum necessaria sit intentio seu petitio recipientis juxta illius Jacobi . . . non tamen semper sit formalis necessaria, sed virtualis seu interpretativa sufficiat.[70]

Cappello proffers several examples of what could constitute an implicit request for the sacraments—if the sick person would receive Holy Viaticum devoutly, if he would ask that a priest be summoned to his bedside, if he gave manifest signs of his

[69] *Extreme Unction,* p. 252.

[70] Suarez, *Commentarius, De Extremo Unctione,* Disp. XLII, sect. 1, n. 6.

sorrow for sin, if he openly stated his desire to die as a Catholic.[71]

It has been demonstrated that a habitual intention suffices for the reception of extreme unction. It remains now to answer the question whether even some lesser form of an intention could suffice, or whether the habitual intention is required.

De Lugo reported without closer identification some authors who objected that no intention was required for the reception of extreme unction, which view they based upon the fact that the Church by way of common practice conferred this sacrament upon those who had lost the use of reason as the result of a sudden illness. In such cases it manifestly was often unlikely that there was in evidence any earlier request for this sacrament.[72]

On the other hand, St. Alphonsus clearly declared that for the sacrament of extreme unction an interpretative intention suffices. Furthermore, he declared this to be the common teaching of the authors.[73]

The opinion of those who denied the necessity of any intention has been refuted earlier. The answer to their objection that those who suddenly are taken ill cannot have an intention will be given in subsequent paragraphs. Beyond this, it is the opinion held by St. Alphonsus which might cause us momentary surprise. On the one hand, we know that St. Alphonsus held it to be incontrovertible that an intention is necessary for all the sacraments without exception. On the other hand, the definition and concept of an interpretative intention as given to us by this same author indicates his own judgment that this was in fact no intention at all, for he wrote:

> Intentio interpretativa habetur cum quis nullam habet nec habuit intentionem actualem, sed ita est dispositus ut si adverteret, haberet.[74]

The solution to the difficulty can be found when one closely examines the terminology that was commonly employed by the writers of that period, a terminology which still finds followers

[71] *De Sacramentis,* III, n. 261.

[72] *De Sacramentis in Genere,* Disp. ix, n. 122.

[73] *Theologia Moralis,* Lib. VI, n. 82.

[74] *Theologia Moralis,* Lib. VI, n. 15.

to this day. When certain authors, e.g., Lacroix, Laymann, De Lugo, Pruemmer, speak of an interpretative intention, they do not mean that intention which a person in fact never had, i.e., an intention which he would have elicited, had he only adverted to its need. Rather, they are speaking of that intention which by an interpretation of certain facts is presumed to be actually present here and now.[75]

Canon 943 then proceeds to consider the case envisioned by the authors whom De Lugo mentioned. It is the case of those for whom through sudden illness or any other cause there is precluded the manifestation of any desire for this sacrament, the while they were still in possession of their senses. However, as Lacroix pointed out, unlike the sacraments of penance and matrimony, extreme unction does not require that a sensible sign have been given by the recipient in order that the sacrament may be validly administered.[76] De Lugo wrote in a similar vein:

> In quo est differentia a sacramento Extremae Unctionis et aliis similibus ad quorum valorem sufficeret voluntas interna, etiamsi exterius non ostenderetur.[77]

Hence it is possible that the sick person, though now bereft of his senses, has previously internally elicited either an explicit or an implicit intention for extreme unction, to which intention he has never given external expression. If the intention has never been retracted, it remains as a habitual intention, and this suffices for the reception of the sacrament.

The law then provides that in those situations wherein it is very likely that the sick person would have requested the sacrament in an external fashion, if he had only adverted to its usefulness in this hour of great spiritual need, a sufficient intention is to be considered as present. Hence it further enjoins an obligation upon the minister to confer the sacrament apart from the appending of any condition (*absolute praebeatur*).

Canon 943, accordingly, cannot be cited as proving the ade-

[75] Iorio, *Theologia Moralis,* I, n. 17.

[76] *Theologia Moralis,* Lib. VI, n. 177.

[77] *De Sacramentis in Genere,* Disp. ix, n. 124.

quacy of an interpretative intention; it serves simply to show that the "interpretative manifestation of an internal implicit habitual intention suffices for the administration of Extreme Unction." [78]

It remains now to determine the facts by the interpretation of which one can rightly presume the existence of an intention to receive extreme unction. An intention is an act of the will, and as such is a purely internal act. Others can come to know of its existence only when it finds some sort of external manifestation. This can take place through a direct statement, either explicit or implicit, as was noted above. It can be made known equally well through some external actions. Thus the Catholic who has received the sacraments with regularity, who has lived up to the laws of the Church, who has made external profession of his faith in these and many other ways, must certainly be presumed to have the desire to receive the sacraments and such other spiritual helps as the Church is ready mercifully to bestow upon the dying. De Lugo expressed it thus:

> Qui enim christianus est et vult in Ecclesia catholica vivere et mori, vult etiam ejus sacramentis debito tempore juvari; quam voluntatem Ecclesia praesumit de omnibus qui signa poenitentiae tempore suo exhibuerunt.[79]

Elsewhere he wrote in a similar fashion:

> Homo christianus ex vi illius voluntatis generalis vult quidem sumere sacramenta more christiano, quando scilicet debito tempore Christianis dari solent, atque ideo habuit jam voluntatem accipiendi extremam unctionem . . . in mortis periculo.[80]

DeConinck (1571-1633), too, held that a previous Catholic life constitutes sufficient evidence of an intention to receive the sacrament. Therefore he placed an obligation upon the minister to confer the sacrament, even though the recipient had been unable, as a result of the suddenness of his illness, to request the sacrament.

[78] Abbo-Hannan, *The Sacred Canons,* II (St. Louis: Herder, 1952), p. 64.

[79] *De Sacramentis in Genere,* Disp. ix, n. 122.

[80] *Ibid.,* n. 127.

> Qui catholice vivit, censetur velle sibi morienti conferri sacramenta ab Ecclesia morientibus conferri solita; idemque si subito desituatur usu rationis, debet inungi.[81]

This presumption when based upon a person's previous Catholic way of life, namely that there is present an intention sufficient for the reception of the sacrament, is especially strong in regard to extreme unction. As LaCroix pointed out:

> Maxime de extrema unctione praesumitur haec voluntas quia, cum sit postremum sacramentum et homines communiter tum non possint eam petere, merito praesumitur omnes eam velle, nisi de contraria voluntate constet.[82]

On the other hand, to limit the application of this presumption solely to those who have lived solidly Catholic lives seems much too severe. In a matter of such great moment, when the salvation of souls hangs in the balance, certainly a benign and merciful approach is indicated. Hence Cappello argues that such an intention is to be presumed as present on the part of all the faithful, not only among those who have lived exemplary Catholic lives, but also among those who have been somewhat lax in the practice of their faith, in fact, even among those who apparently have been only nominal Catholics.[83]

In this conclusion he finds support in the person of Benedict XIV, who wrote:

> De quolibet fideli de quo contrarium non constat, praesumendum est fuisse hoc sacramentum petiturum, si potuisset; passim siquidem videmus, Extremam Unctionem muniri, qui subita vi morbi oppressi, sensibus destituuntur, nec ullum Sacramenti desiderium significare valent: eorum quippe perspecta pietas et fides, non obscurum praebet argumentum desiderii, quod, si possent, demonstrarent.[84]

81 DeConinck as quoted by Gaudé, in St. Alphonsus, *Theologia Moralis,* Lib. VI, n. 82, note b.

82 *Theologia Moralis,* Lib. VI, n. 171.

83 "Proinde quilibet fidelis, de quo contrarium non constat, praesumitur sacramentum petiturus, si potuisset."—*De Sacramentis,* III (3. ed., Taurini: Marietti, 1949), n. 264 (3).

84 *De Synodo Dioecesana,* Lib. VIII, c. 6, n. 5.

2. Obstinate Impenitence Indicates the Absence of an Intention

Canon 942, however, indicates one instance wherein we may feel certain of the absence of even an implicit habitual intention.

> Hoc sacramentum non est conferendum illis qui impoenitentes in manifesto peccato mortali contumaciter perseverant; quod si hoc dubium fuerit, conferatur sub conditione.

For the application of the provisions of this canon five conditions must be verified. "The subject must be 1) obstinate and contumacious in 2) his impenitence with regard to a 3) manifest 4) mortal sin; while the minister must 5) have certainty with regard to the existence of this soul-condition of the subject." [85]

The slightest doubt on the part of the minister in regard to the presence of any of these conditions will warrant at least a conditional administration of the sacrament. Cappello, summing up these same requirements, but under only two heads, notes that this canon will as a result seldom find application.

> Haec duplex conditio, in praxi, numquam aut fere numquam omnimoda certitudine verificatur. Nam, quamdiu Titius vivit, etsi sensus amittat, ex motu gratiae divinae nonne potest actum doloris interius elicere atque a prava voluntate recedere? Igitur sacramentum extremae unctionis potest, imo debet, in tali casu ministrari.[86]

Hence it is only in the most extreme cases that the minister of the sacrament will be unable legitimately to presume the presence of a sufficient intention on the part of one who is professedly a Catholic.

A number of authors, however, prefer to see a penal aspect in this canon, and thus believe that the denial of the sacrament must be looked upon as a punishment, "a well-deserved—yea, necessary—punishment." The punishment is well-deserved, since such an impenitent, obstinate sinner despises the sacraments and the Church's means of grace, or otherwise he would amend his ways. The punishment is necessary, because under such conditions the sacrament would be frustrated and dishon-

[85] Kilker, *Extreme Unction,* p. 229.

[86] *De Sacramentis,* III, n. 263.

ored.[87] Others who espouse a similar view include Blat (1867-1943),[88] Tanquerey (1854-1932),[89] Kilker (1901-1944),[90] and, apparently in his earlier editions, Vermeersch (1858-1936).

The more common view, however, holds that this canon is concerned with the absence of the requisite intention, which absence is made manifest by the contumacious perseverance in sin on the part of the sick person. McCarthy writes: "The absence of an intention is manifested by or is implied in his impenitent contumacious perseverance in manifest mortal sin." [91]

Other recent authors who prefer this latter opinion are Noldin,[92] Vermeersch,[93] Iorio,[94] Cappello,[95] Merkelbach,[96] and Coronata.[97]

In support of this latter view these writers appeal to the commonly accepted theological principle that conditions are to be appended in the administration of the sacraments only when there exists a prudent doubt in regard to those matters which concern the substantial nature of the sacrament, and thus its valid conferring. Conditions are not to be employed when there are doubts in regard to the dispositions of the recipient, since this would eliminate the possibility of a later reviviscence of the sacrament, should the disposition of the subject improve.

87 Pruemmer, "The Recipient of Extreme Unction according to the Code," *The Homiletic and Pastoral Review*, XXVI (1926), 740-741.

88 *Commentarium Textus Codicis Iuris Canonici*, Lib. III, Pars I (2. ed., Romae, 1924), n. 286.

89 *Synopsis Theologiae Dogmaticae*, Vol. III (24. ed., Benziger: New York, 1938), n. 974.

90 *Extreme Unction*, p. 227.

91 *Irish Ecclesiastical Record*, 5. Series, LXVI (1945), 369.

92 *Summa Theologiae Moralis*, III, n. 443 (3).

93 *Theologia Moralis*, III, n. 614; cf. also Vermeersch-Creusen, *Epitome Iuris Canonici*, II (7. ed., Mechliniae-Romae: Dessain, 1954), n. 226.

94 *Theologia Moralis*, III, n. 766.

95 *De Sacramentis*, III, n. 263.

96 *Summa Theologiae Moralis*, III, n. 705.

97 *De Sacramentis*, I, n. 552.

> Conditio apponenda est illa quae respicit validitatem sacramenti, non vero illa quae respicit dispositionem ad sacramenti fructum, quia non est impedienda sacramenti reviviscentia. Hoc est generale principium quod valet pro omnibus sacramentis; unde Extrema Unctio conferatur sub conditione: *si es capax,* vel alia simili, non sub conditione: *si es dispositus.* Nec existimetur in can. 942 huic regulae poni exceptionem, quia in illis qui in manifesto peccato contumaciter perseverant, iam non potest cum aliqua probabilitate supponi intentio recipiendi sacramentum; unde si de hac contumacia dubium sit, pariter dubium erit de intentione, non de sola dispositione. Valet proinde regula generalis.[98]

F. An Implicit Intention Suffices for Holy Orders

With the assumption of holy orders the recipient undertakes a whole series of new and most serious obligations. With this sacrament there comes a complete change of status. He is no longer just a member of Christ's Church; he is a member of its hierarchy. To him in a special manner are addressed the words of Christ, the commands to teach, to baptize, to pursue a life of pre-eminent holiness. Moreover, there is imprinted upon his soul the unerasable sacramental character of the sacrament. Thus his new status is not one which he can shed at will, but rather it will continue and persist in perpetuity.

Because of these serious burdens which are intrinsically bound up with the acquisition of holy orders, and also on account of this complete change in status, it seems reasonable to believe that an implicit intention such as that which is sufficient for extreme unction will not be likewise sufficient for the reception of this sacrament. For many writers, then, an implicit intention is not considered enough for a valid reception of holy orders; an explicit intention is demanded by them.[99]

Moreover, the sacrament of holy orders is not one of those sacraments which is necessary for salvation. Hence it is not ad-

[98] Merkelbach, *Summa Theologiae Moralis,* III, n. 705 (6); cf. also Iorio, *Theologia Moralis,* III, n. 18.

[99] "Ad ordinem non sufficit interpretativa, cum enim Ordo sit immutatio totius status afferatque onera illi. . . ."—Lacroix, *Theologia Moralis,* Lib. VI, n. 173.

ministered to the faithful in general, but only to those who desire it and have previously shown themselves worthy. Therefore, the general intention which all Catholics are assumed to have to live and to die in the Catholic Church and to receive those sacraments which the Church bestows at the appropriate time does not imply or include the reception of holy orders. This general intention, in which an intention for the sacraments is implicitly contained, carries within itself this specific implication in regard to only those sacraments which are customarily given to the dying.

> Voluntas generalis, quam prius habuit suscipiendi sacramenta, non fuit voluntas suscipiendi omnia sacramenta, sed ea solum, quae Christianis communiter dari solent tamquam remedia communia.[100]

Thus the great majority of authors insist that an explicit intention is demanded for the valid reception of holy orders, e.g., St. Alphonsus,[101] Cappello,[102] Coronata,[103] Pruemmer,[104] Vermeersch,[105] and Iorio.[106]

Other writers, however, believe that inherently an implicit habitual intention will suffice for all of the sacraments. In practice, however, it may be difficult to uncover an intention which is so general as implicitly to include a desire to receive holy orders. This seems to be the understanding of Merkelbach who wrote: "Intentio requisita est habitualis . . . et quidem *per se* sufficit habitualis implicita suscipiendi sacramentum. . . ,"[107] whereas later he stated: "At talis voluntas [habitualis implicita] non sufficit, sed explicita requiritur: b) ad Ordinem et Matri-

[100] De Lugo, *De Sacramentis in Genere,* Disp. ix, n. 127.

[101] *Theologia Moralis,* Lib. VI, n. 82.

[102] *De Sacramentis,* I, n. 74 (5).

[103] *De Sacramentis,* I, n. 93.

[104] *Manuale Theologiae Moralis,* III, n. 87.

[105] *Theologia Moralis,* III, n. 185.

[106] *Theologia Moralis,* III, n. 35 (5).

[107] *Summa Theologiae Moralis,* III, n. 93.

monium, in quibus novus status cum novis officiis est suscipiendus."[108] Connell writes in a similar fashion:

> . . . non negatur principium generale supra statutum de sufficientia intentionis implicitae in subjecto, sed tantum asseritur nullas vel paucas esse intentiones generales quae in se inclusas habeant voluntatem haec sacramenta recipiendi.[109]

Therefore, it would seem that one can admit that an implicit habitual intention will in all cases be sufficient for the valid reception of the sacraments.[110]

[108] *Ibid.*, n. 94.

[109] *De Sacramentis Ecclesiae,* n. 61.

[110] Noldin, *Summa Theologiae Moralis,* III, n. 41 (5); Genicot-Salsmans, *Institutiones Theologiae Moralis,* II, n. 126; Doronzo, *De Sacramentis in Genere,* p. 335.

CHAPTER VI

THE EXTENT OF THE IMPLICIT HABITUAL INTENTION IS LIMITED

It has been established with certainty that an implicit habitual intention will suffice for the valid reception of the sacraments when the subject is in danger of death. At such times the simple fact that the person is a Catholic and has lived a Catholic life is viewed as constituting a sufficient basis for assuming the presence of the required intention. Bucceroni (1841-1918) implied that this same general intention to receive the sacraments might suffice for the valid and fruitful reception of the Eucharist at other times as well.[1] The question which remains is whether the efficacy of this general intention may possibly be extended so as to cover other situations wherein the subject is temporarily without the use of his senses, e.g., while he is asleep, drunk, etc.

According to St. Alphonsus, Roncaglia (1677-1737) denied the validity of any sacrament which was administered to persons who were completely drunk, who were asleep, or who were insane, even though they had earlier elicited an intention to receive the sacrament.[2] Gaudé (1860-1910), in his edition of St. Alphonsus' work, modified this statement by pointing out that Roncaglia held for the invalidity of the sacrament in only those cases wherein the person was asleep or drunk. He did not, therefore, apply this same judgment in regard to those who had become insane, nor, of course, to the sick who were destitute of their senses.[3] Roncaglia denied the validity of the sacraments when they were conferred on the sleeping or upon the drunk, for he felt that it could not legitimately be presumed that these persons had an intention to receive these sacred rites at such a time and together with such material irreverence. Rather, he

[1] *Institutiones Theologiae Moralis,* Vol. III (6. ed., Romae, 1915), n. 383.

[2] *Theologia Moralis,* Lib. VI, n. 81.

[3] St. Alphonsus, *Theologia Moralis,* Lib. VI, n. 81, note f.

believed that it should be presumed that they desired to receive the sacraments only in the way in which they are customarily given and received in the Catholic community.

> Non est praesumendum eos habuisse intentionem in tali tempore recipiendi sacramentum, sed solummodo more et ritu Christiano.[4]

Roncaglia was not alone in holding this view, for Sporer was another author who also rejected the validity of the sacraments when they were conferred upon those who were not in danger of death or in other spiritual distress.

> Haec tamen generalis intentio minime efficit quod alicui Christiano valide conferatur extrema unctio vel Confirmatio aut fructuose sumatur Eucharistia in somno, ebrietate, vel amentia temporali. . . . Quia . . . generalis voluntas minime se extendit ad casus quibus Christiano more sacramenta dari non solent nec debent ut in somno, ebrietate, temporali furore vel amentia. . . .[5]

He reaffirmed this teaching in regard also to confirmation.

> Longe probabilius non sufficit ad suscipiendam confirmationem extra periculum mortis vel perpetuam amentiam vel valde diu duratam.[6]

Furthermore, he pointed out that even though the recipient was a Catholic and had up to that time lived a devout Catholic life, one could not presume from these facts that he had an intention to receive confirmation at that time, when there was no immediate need of the sacrament. Rather, it seemed a more reasonable presumption that he intended to receive the sacrament while possessing the actual use of reason and with the necessary reverence which the sacrament demands.[7]

Billuart (1685-1757) also held the administration of at least baptism, confirmation and orders under such circumstances to be invalid, despite the presence of a habitual intention. This

[4] St. Alphonsus, *Theologia Moralis,* Lib. VI, n. 81.

[5] *Theologia Moralis Sacramentalis,* Pars I, c. 2, sect. 3, n. 155.

[6] *Ibid.,* n. 156.

[7] *Loc. cit.*

held true, however, only if the recipient had not previously made an express intention to receive the sacraments even at such an inappropriate time.[8]

Lehmkuhl (1834-1918) indicated at least some doubt about the validity of any sacrament when administered to a sleeping person or to someone in a similar state.

> Non intelligo indubie valere sacramenta quae utcunque post illam intentionem dormienti etc. conferantur. Valent utique in casu necessitatis quando timendum est ne alias homo sacramentum non amplius possit recipere, siquidem intentio recipiendi aliquando sacramenti includit prorsus voluntatem illud recipiendi in periculo mortis quando antea intentio non fuerit impleta; sed num includat etiam voluntatem utcumque quolibet tempore absque conscientia sui sacramentum extra necessitatem recipiendi, non est plane certum.[9]

According to St. Alphonsus, Roncaglia, in holding this opinion, stood apart from the great majority of the writers, who defended the validity of the sacraments conferred under such circumstances. Such authors as De Lugo, the Salmanticenses, LaCroix, Gobat, and Benedict XIV were cited by St. Alphonsus as holding that under such circumstances the sacraments were conferred validly. Hence St. Alphonsus termed their opinion as being held "communissime et probabilius."[10]

These authors argued that in this regard no more is required to make the recipient a fit subject, that is, one capable of receiving the sacrament, than that there be present a habitual consent to receive the sacrament. The presence of an implicit habitual intention can be legitimately presumed from the fact that the person is a Catholic and leads a Catholic life. This furnishes a sufficient basis for acknowledging the presence of such an intention in the case of the dying. There seems not to be any reason for denying its equal applicability in this situation.

Moreover, the fact that the recipient is drunk, or asleep, or

[8] *De Sacramentis in Communi,* Diss. VI, n. 1.

[9] *Theologia Moralis,* II, n. 48.

[10] *Institutiones Theologiae Moralis,* II, n. 384.

suffering from temporary insanity, is a purely accidental circumstance. The intention of the recipient is not such as to allow for a modification or limitation in view of such accidentals.[11]

Finally, these writers appeal to the authority of Innocent III and Benedict XIV. Innocent III in his decretal letter, *Maiores,* acknowledged the validity of the baptism of the *dormientes,* if they had earlier elicited an intention to receive baptism.

> Secus autem si prius (dormientes et amentes) catechumeni exstitissent, et habuissent propositum baptizandi; unde tales in necessitatis articulo consuevit ecclesia baptizare.[12]

A similar view was held by Benedict XIV according to the supporters of this second opinion.

> Hic casus ad eos spectat, qui ante furorem, vel somnum, baptismum petunt, accipiunt vero, dum aut insania vexantur, aut somno indulgent, et hoc genus hominum valide baptizantum dicitur in Conc. III Carthagin., cap. 34.[13]

It seems certain that when the recipient of the sacrament has earlier made an explicit intention to receive the sacrament, e.g., confirmation, that this intention will suffice to render him a fit subject for a valid reception of the sacrament regardless of the attending circumstances. No qualifications seem contained in such an intention. No limitations seem to be placed, so that the intention is to be regarded as covering every eventuality. It seems that both Innocent III and Benedict XIV considered precisely the case wherein the subject had previously manifested some desire to receive the sacrament. In both cases, so it appears, some sort of explicit request had preceded.

The same however, is not true when one examines the implicit intention as contained in a man's previous life as a Catholic. This implicit intention is understood by the authors to be contained in the more generic desire which all Catholics have to live and die as Catholics. Included in this general intention, then,

[11] "Nobis vero melior videtur sententia, quam defendit Gasparri, intentionem suscipientis non se extendere ad circumstantias accidentales. . . ."—Connell, *De Sacramentis Ecclesiae,* n. 61.

[12] C. 3, X, *de baptismo et eius effectu,* III, 42.

[13] Ep. *Postremo mense,* 28 febr. 1747, n. 46—*Fontes,* n. 377.

is the more specific intention to receive those sacraments which the Church is wont to confer upon its children, and at the time and under the circumstances in which it customarily grants them.

> Homo christianus ex vi illius voluntatis generalis vult quidem sumere sacramenta more Christiano, quando scilicet debito tempore christianis dari solent. . . .[14]

Hence, though under a different aspect the time and the circumstances of the administration of the sacraments may seem to be purely accessory to the recipient's intention, they seem to form an integral part of the general intention which every Catholic is presumed to possess. Accordingly, the implicit habitual intention appears not to have an unlimited application; it appears to apply in only those cases wherein the danger of death or of perpetual insanity is present.[15]

[14] De Lugo, *De Sacramentis in Genere,* Disp. ix, n. 127.

[15] "Extra periculum mortis vel amentiam perpetuam non praesumi voluntatem suscipiendi confirmationem, quia plerique potius volunt sumere cum usu rationis."—Laymann, *Theologia Moralis,* Lib. VI, n. 169.

CHAPTER VII

AN INTERNAL INTENTION IS REQUIRED FOR THE VALIDITY OF THE SACRAMENTS

A. Gasparri Taught That an External Intention Suffices

The late Cardinal Gasparri (1852-1934) provided new fuel for controversy when he supported the opinion that external consent is of itself sufficient for the valid reception of holy orders. This opinion is not entirely new. It had previously been favored by Drouin (1682-1742). The situation as it was visualized by Gasparri was one wherein the young ordinand in approaching the ordaining prelate externally manifests the same willingness to receive orders as the others about him, but internally very certainly is unwilling to receive the sacrament. The young man in the case simply permits and allows in his regard the conferring of the sacred rites by the bishop, but he withholds his inward consent for the reception of the order.

Cardinal Gasparri based his view principally on the words of the decretal *Maiores* of Pope Innocent III. Pope Innocent III first set forth the opinion held by some contemporary authors:

> Sunt autem nonnulli, qui dicunt quod sacramenta quae per se sortiuntur effectum, ut baptismus et ordo ceteraque similia, non solum dormientibus et amentibus, sed invitis etiam et contradicentibus, etsi non quantum ad rem, quantum tamen ad characterem conferuntur, cum non solum parvuli, qui non consentiunt, sed et ficti, qui quam non ore, corde tamen dissentiunt, recipiant sacramentum.[1]

Innocent III rejected this opinion as being untenable in view of the fact that in its consequences it would be contrary to the practice of the Church. Then he proceeded to set forth the teaching of a second group.

[1] C. 3, X, *de baptismo et eius effectu,* III, 42.

> Propter quod inter invitum et invitum, coactum et coactum, alii non absurde distinguunt, quod is, qui terroribus atque suppliciis violenter attrahitur, et, ne detrimentum incurrat, baptismi suscipit sacramentum, talis, sicut et is qui ficte ad baptismum accedit, characterem suscipit christianitatis impressum.[2]

Despite the effort of Many (1847-1922) to limit the approval given by Innocent III solely to the distinction made between the various kinds of compulsion,[3] authors generally acknowledge that the Pope truly presented his own views on the matter.[4]

Insincerity (*fictio*), then, was understood in the sense of those who did not manifest externally their unwillingness to receive baptism, "ficti, qui quam non ore, corde tamen dissentiunt." Despite this contradiction between their external behavior and their inward desires, the sacrament was acknowledged as being validly received, "is qui ficte ad baptismum accedit, characterem suscipit christianitatis impressum."

This was also the understanding reflected in the gloss to this very decretal, which states that only when the insincerity has been banished will the sacrament be received fruitfully as well as validly.

> Illi (ficti) ore exprimunt, licet corde dissentiant, et ideo sacramentum recipiunt, quia Ecclesia dare intendit; sed tale sacramentum non prodest ad remissionem peccatorum, nisi cum fictio illa recesserit.[5]

Gasparri reasoned that in the approach of the ordinand there is manifest a desire for the sacrament, since he wants the application of the matter and the form by a minister who possesses the required intention. However, since he is approaching insincerely, he does not desire the effects of the sacrament, namely the sacramental character and grace. Now, the principal effect of the sacrament, the character, is always produced *ex opere operato,*

[2] C. 3, X, *de baptismo et eius effectu,* III, 42.

[3] *Praelectiones de Sacra Ordinatione* (Parisiis, 1905), p. 597.

[4] Gasparri, *Tractatus Canonicus de Sacra Ordinatione,* Vol. I (Parisiis, 1893), n. 643.

[5] *Glossa Ord.* ad c. 3, X, *de baptismo et eius effectu,* III, 42, s.v. *perdurare.*

as long as the person is a fit subject and has an intention of receiving the sacrament. Hence, so Gasparri concluded, despite his own unwillingness the person in question validly receives holy orders, baptism or confirmation.[6]

Moreover, in this case, the candidate would possess two contrary intentions. The first intention is to receive the sacrament because he has approached the minister of the sacrament; the second intention is not to receive it. Since he has approached, it is the first intention which prevails and makes the sacrament valid.[7]

B. Authors Commonly Require an Internal Intention

There can be no doubt, as Gasparri himself admitted, that this opinion goes against the almost unanimous teaching of the other authors. Yet Gasparri seemed unimpressed by this unanimity; he reminded the reader of the undeniable practice of writers, namely of copying their material without having given lengthy or serious consideration to the matter.[8]

By his own admission, Gasparri relied most heavily on the decretal *Maiores* in support for his conclusions. In reply authors first point out that Innocent III mentions the first listed opinion only in order to reject it entirely. Hence it should not be used as the basis for argument.[9]

Moreover, a number of authors believe that Innocent III employed the term *fictio* in a dual sense. When he adverted to the first opinion, which he immediately refuted, he implied an inner lack of intention. However, when he later again used the same term he dealt with a lack of the requisite dispositions.[10] This second use of the term *fictio* was unquestionably a common one at that time. An adequate and satisfactory definition for insincerity can be found already in the *Decretum* of Gratian:

[6] *Tractatus Canonicus de Sacra Ordinatione,* I, n. 645.

[7] *Loc. cit.*

[8] *Loc. cit.*

[9] Cappello, *De Sacramentis,* IV (2. ed., Taurini: Marietti, 1947), n. 361 (5).

[10] Many, *Praelectiones de Sacra Ordinatione,* p. 597; Cappello, *De Sacramentis,* IV, n. 361 (5); Coronata, *De Sacramentis,* II (2. ed., Taurini: Marietti, 1949), n. 65.

> Tunc valere incipit ad salutem baptismus, cum illa fictio veraci confessione recesserit, quae, *corde in malitia vel sacrilegio perseverante,* peccatorum ablutionem non sinebat fieri.[11]

This interpretation of the term insincerity, as referring to disposition rather than to intention, is bolstered by the citing of several passages in the Gloss, wherein the terms insincerity (*ficte*) and without contrition (*sine contritione*) are regarded as synonymous. Thus we find these words: "Si quis adultus fictus vel sine contritione accedit ad baptismum. . . ." [12] Hostiensis also clearly understood insincerity as referring to a lack of proper disposition at the time when the sacrament is received. He wrote: "Si aliquis adultus baptismum accepit ficte, scilicet quia non conterat quando recipit. . . ." [13]

Finally, there may here be restated the doctrine of St. Thomas, who declared that a person could approach the sacrament insincerely in four ways:

> First, when he does not believe, whereas baptism is the very sacrament of faith; secondly, through scorning the sacrament itself; thirdly, through observing a rite which differs from the one prescribed by the Church in conferring the sacrament; fourthly, through approaching the sacrament without devotion.[14]

It is in this fourth sense that the canonical writers preferred to understand the term, i.e., in the meaning of a lack of the requisite devotion or disposition, rather than as a lack of the required intention. Thus, as long as insincerity was understood in this sense, there could be no question as to the validity of the sacrament. Hostiensis, for one, declared that baptism, if conferred on one who is insincere, is valid, but he pointed out that, though the character of the sacrament is received, grace is not.[15] Only when

[11] C. 42, D. IV, *de cons.;* cf. also c. 32, D. IV, *de cons.*

[12] *Glossa Ord.* ad c. 35, C. I, q. 1, s.v. *sicut ficte;* also *Glossa Ord.* ad c. 3, X, *de baptismo et eius effectu,* III, 42, s.v. *sicut ficte.*

[13] *Summa Aurea,* Lib. III, tit. 42, n. 15.

[14] *Summa Theologica,* III, q. 69, a. 9, in corp.

[15] "Characterem recipiunt (ficti), sed non rem sacramenti."—*Summa Aurea,* Lib. III, tit. 42, n. 12.

the insincerity was removed by way of contrition or sorrow for sin, could grace be infused and the sins which stained the soul be forgiven.[16]

St. Thomas, too, after outlining the four kinds of insincerity, declared that "it is evident that insincerity hinders the effect of baptism." [17] However, there was no doubt that the baptism was valid, and when the obstacle of insincerity was removed by way of penance, baptism forthwith produced its effect of grace as well.[18]

Doronzo, however, denies that the term insincerity (*fictio*) is to be understood in this twofold sense in the Decretal. Certainly, to say that Innocent III, an eminent and highly skilled jurist, used the same term in two different senses in the same paragraph is most difficult to accept. Doronzo, therefore, believed that in both places the term must be understood as it was explained by the Pope: "ficti, qui quamvis non ore, corde tamen dissentiunt." [19]

According to Doronzo, Innocent III's words need not be understood as indicating a complete lack or absence of an intention. Rather, he contemplated simply the lack of a full and complete intention. In the same context he treated of those who by threats and violence are compelled to receive baptism. Their baptism was valid, for they had given some consent, though not a full consent. According to Doronzo, then, the Pope used this as a parallel case, indicating that some degree of consent may be present in one who is insincere.[20]

Finally, Innocent IV (1243-1254), when writing some fifty years later and commenting on the words of his predecessor, Innocent III, interpretated his text in such a way as to reflect the conviction that a mere external consent is insufficient for the valid reception of a sacrament.

[16] "Si aliquis adultus baptismum accepit ficte, scilicet quia non conterat, quando recipit, licet character in eum imprimatur, non tamen gratia nec remittuntur peccata, sed tunc demum incipit operari cum fictio recedit."—Hostiensis, *Summa Aurea,* Lib. III, tit. 42, n. 15.

[17] *Summa Theologica,* III, q. 69, a. 9.

[18] *Ibid.,* a. 10.

[19] Doronzo, *De Sacramentis in Genere,* p. 348.

[20] *Loc. cit.*

> Sed quid si baptizatus petiit baptismum sed baptizari non intendebat, nec aliquid per baptismum conferri? Et videtur quod non sit baptizatus, quia numquam consensit baptizari . . . licet verba consensus exprimat.[21]

Yet, despite the great mass of argumentation mustered by himself and others in seeking to obviate the force of the arguments drawn by Gasparri from the decretal of Innocent III, Many nevertheless seemed in the end to confess that his rebuttal remained inconclusive. Accordingly he wrote:

> Fatendum tamen est, ne quid urgeatur, aliquam remanere difficultatem circa mentem Innocentii III . . . unde, ad summum, non habemus nisi opinionem privatam Innocentii III, quam etiam coaetanei rejecerunt.[22]

Gasparri cited in his favor the later teaching of Benedict XIV, as expressed in the Epistle *Postremo mense,* February 28, 1747, and claimed at least the neutrality of the Pope, if not his outright support. He acknowledged that in an earlier work Prosper Lambertini had sided with the common opinion. In his earlier work, *Commentarius de Sacrosancto Missae Sacrificio,* Benedict XIV had written: "Certissimum illud remanet, ei, qui re ipsa contradixerit, nullum characterem fuisse impressum, actumque totum invalidum esse."[23] Though Benedict XIV in his Epistle *Postremo mense* totally and utterly rejected the opinion of Catharinus (1483-1553) in regard to the question of the intention of the minister, he acknowledged that in regard to the intention of the recipient there was less difficulty in admitting this view.[24]

However, elsewhere in the very same epistle Benedict XIV considered the exact case in question, and aligned himself on the side of those who denied the validity of the sacrament. First he described the case: "Qui vultu, atque oculis, ac toto corpore ad modestiam composito, voluntate tamen alienissima, ad hoc sacramentum veniat. . . ."[25] After a lengthly discussion of the case,

[21] Lib. III, tit. 42, c. 1, n. 10.

[22] *Praelectiones de Sacra Ordinatione,* p. 597, note 5.

[23] Tom. II (Lovanii, 1762), Sect. II, n. 79.

[24] Ep. *Postremo mense,* n. 47—*Fontes,* n. 377.

[25] *Loc. cit.*

he suggested that the person himself be carefully questioned about his intention at the time. As a result of this questioning, one might discover that the person had no desire at all to receive the sacrament. In this case the person was to be urged to receive the sacrament properly this second time, and it was to be administered to him without the placing of any condition, since the previous baptism was obviously invalid.

> Quod si nulla sit reliqua dubitatio, planeque constet hac luce clarius, adulto baptismum accipiendi nullam prorsus fuisse voluntatem, aut intentionem, nil restat aliud, quam eundem et hortari, et admonere, ut rite id faciat, quod iam irrito fecit, et suscipiat *absolute,* ac libere sacramentum; ac si obstinate repugnet, tum nihil aliud superest, nisi ut remittatur.[26]

As Gasparri himself admitted, the same teaching can be applied with equal cogency to holy orders.[27]

In regard to marriage, canon 1086 declares that the general presumption of law will be that a person's external acts are in conformity with his internal state of mind. At the same time it acknowledges that, despite an external show of consent, an inwardly true matrimonial consent could be withheld. This is not an attempt to apply this same doctrine to holy orders, but at least it is evident that, when there exist two contrary intentions, it is not the external intention, but rather the internal intention which prevails.

Moreover, as Cappello pointed out, it is in utter contradiction of all sound philosophical principles to say that the external intention is the one which we must look to, if there is any disagreement between it and the internal dispositions of the intellect and will.[28] To say that to intend to allow the external sacramental rites to be performed over oneself is the same as to intend to receive the sacrament is also most difficult to accept.

For these reasons, then, virtually all authors have insisted that it is not enough to consent to the external sacramental actions, but this kind of consent must be accompanied by internal consent to receive the sacrament itself.

[26] *Ibid.,* n. 51—*Fontes,* n. 377.

[27] *Tractatus Canonicus de Sacra Ordinatione,* I, n. 645.

[28] *De Sacramentis,* IV, n. 361 (6).

> Hoc autem intelligi debet, dummodo internus sit verus consensus in sacramentum, non vero si solus sit consensus in actionem externam absque alio consensu interno in ipsum sacramentum.[29]

Billuart, in commenting on the words of St. Thomas, also insisted that the intention must have as its object the receiving of the sacrament as something sacred in the Church. He rejected the view which held for the validity of the sacraments when they are received in mere sport, with simulation, or as some profane object.[30] Because of its opposition to the common teaching, Pope Gregory XIII (1572-1585) ordered the following gloss to Innocent III expunged: "Valere sacramentum ab eo susceptum, qui corde dissentit, modo dicat se ore consentire." [31]

Finally, Cappello cites several decisions of the Roman Congregations which seem to lend support to his conclusions. In view of the mass of evidence opposed to the opinion of Cardinal Gasparri, it seems that the contrary view which regards an ordination as invalid if the ordinand withholds internal consent is to be accepted with certainty. Hence the suggestion of Gasparri that the ordination is to be repeated only conditionally, seems supplanted with the demand for an unconditional repetition.[32]

[29] De Lugo, *De Sacramentis in Genere,* Disp. ix, n. 131.

[30] "Hanc autem intentionem debere esse internam, idest, intentionem suscipiendi rem ut sacram in Ecclesia, seu quod Ecclesia facit, nec sufficere intentionem recipiendi rem profanam, aut simulandi vel ludendi, est diserte S. Thomae in supplemento . . . et patet quia qui intenderit recipere rem profanam aut simulare vel ludere, non intenderet recipere sacramentum."—*De Sacramentis in Communi,* diss. vi, art. 1.

[31] Cf. Doronzo, *De Sacramentis in Genere,* p. 348.

[32] *Tractatus Canonicus de Sacra Ordinatione,* I, n. 645.

CHAPTER VIII

THE VALIDITY OF THE SACRAMENTS CONFERRED IN THE FACE OF CONTRARY INTENTIONS

A. The Nature and Concept of Contrary Intentions

In the very act of receiving one of the sacraments the recipient may conceivably possess two, or even more, mutually opposed and contrary intentions. The opposition between these two intentions may arise from several sources, for example, from ignorance, from error, or even from mere forgetfulness.[1]

Thus the recipient may intend to receive that baptism which he believes was instituted by Christ himself, while at the same time he wills or intends to exclude the reception of that type of baptism which he knows to be conferred in and by the Catholic Church.[2] Another example would be that of a baptized non-Catholic who wishes to marry another baptized person, and yet at the same time intends to exclude the sacrament of matrimony.

In seeking to determine the validity of the sacraments when they are received with such contrary intentions one may have to advert to several possibilities. The two mutually opposed intentions may nullify each other, thus rendering the entire sacramental act invalid, or one of the intentions may alone prevail, with the resultant possibility of a valid reception of the sacrament. In regard to the latter case, some rule remains to be established before one can succeed in ascertaining which is in fact the prevailing or the predominant intention.

B. The Predominance of One Intention over All Others

The authors commonly assume that, when two contrary intentions are present in the same subject, these two intentions generally are not of equal import, so that the subject in reality prizes the one more highly than the other. The more highly prized

[1] De Lugo, *De Sacramentis in Genere,* Disp. viii, n. 122.

[2] De Lugo, *De Sacramentis in Genere,* Disp. viii, n. 120.

intention is the one which the authors call the *intentio praedominans* or the *intentio praevalens*.[3] If the predominant intention is such that standing alone it would suffice for the valid reception of the sacrament, then, despite the presence of a second contrary intention, this prior intention will prevail and the sacrament is validly received. As de Lugo stated it:

> Regula communis et vera theologorum est ut voluntas quae praevalet ex iis sortiatur effectum.[4]

This is true, for when two such contrary intentions are present, the predominant intention must be considered as containing an explicit or at least an implicit revocation of the other contrary intention.

> Ex quibus omnibus constat, concurrente duplici voluntate contraria, illam praevalere quae explicite vel implicite continet revocationem alterius.[5]

In seeking to determine which of the several contrary intentions is the predominant one, one may well employ the following norm: Strive to determine which intention the recipient of the sacraments would have chosen, had he been aware that the two contrary intentions could not co-exist.[6]

Generally it is to be presumed, unless there are positive indications to the contrary, that the recipient intends to receive the sacrament. All other intentions which accompany this principal intention are to be regarded as accessory, and consequently subject to yielding to the principal intention in case of conflict. The subject is considered always to wish to receive the sacrament as Christ has objectively instituted it, and not as he, the recipient, subjectively conceives it. Hence, when the recipient entertains two contrary intentions, it is the generic intention which in accord

[3] Vermeersch, *Theologia Moralis,* III, n. 166; Pruemmer, *Manuale Theologiae Moralis,* III, n. 66.

[4] *De Sacramentis in Genere,* Disp. viii, n. 120.

[5] De Lugo, *De Sacramentis in Genere,* Disp. viii, n. 122; St. Alphonsus, *Theologia Moralis,* Lib. VI, n. 25.

[6] St. Alphonsus, *Theologia Moralis,* Lib. VI, n. 24; "Intentio praedominans, nempe eam quae eligeretur cognita incompatibilitate."—Pruemmer, *Manuale Theologiae Moralis,* III, n. 66.

with the will of Christ that ordinarily prevails over any other intention which is the product of a purely private erroneous judgment.[7]

Quite generally this will be true. However, there is not ruled out the possibility of a mind particularly warped in religious matters which would in fact prefer not to receive any sacrament rather than, e.g., to receive the type of baptism conferred in and by the Catholic Church. In this case the predominant intention would not be that of receiving what Christ has instituted, and the sacrament would, of course, be invalid in consequence of the lack of a sufficient intention on the part of the recipient.

An examination of the example which was cited earlier together with an application of the principles here suggested may make this matter somewhat clearer. In the example, the recipient of baptism willed in an absolute manner to receive that baptism which was instituted by Christ. At the same time he entertained the intention of excluding that type of baptism which is conferred in and by the Catholic Church. An analysis of these two contrary intentions reveals at once that the second intention has its origin in a most serious dogmatic error. The person erroneously believes that the baptism administered in the Catholic Church cannot be identified with the baptism instituted by Christ. Accordingly he believes that Catholic baptism is something entirely distinct from that which he wishes to receive. Therefore, in good faith, he desires to exclude whatever he in his error considers to be false and inimical to the teaching of the Divine Master.

If, however, his ignorance were dispelled by the light of truth, and if he were made aware of the true state of affairs, namely, that the Catholic baptism is truly the same as that baptism which Christ instituted, then he would most assuredly revoke his second contrary intention at once, allowing only the first to remain. Thus the second intention, though it appears to be absolute and unconditional in its external form, yet in fact it is subordinated to and made dependent upon the first more generic intention.

[7] "Intentio generalis qua vult quod Christus instituit, praevalet intentioni provenienti ex errore privato."—St. Alphonsus, *Theologia Moralis,* Lib. VI, n. 25.

The first intention, indeed, stands as the prevailing, predominant intention. It is the intention which in reality will prevail and will bring about that condition of consent on the part of the recipient which is demanded for a valid reception of the sacrament.

Up to now consideration has been limited to those cases wherein the presence of the contrary intentions has its origin in errors in regard to dogmatic truth. Piscetta-Gennaro give us an example of the presence of contrary intentions which shows that the same principles can be equally well applied when the error concerns some particular fact.[8] Titius is sick and is in danger of death. He has previously asked for and received the Eucharist during his illness. He refuses, however, to allow the priest to confer extreme unction. He insists that he has too much reverence for the sacrament to allow it to be conferred upon himself invalidly, and since he is convinced that he is not in danger of death, he is certain that the sacrament would be invalid. Later Titius lapses into a coma. At this time the priest comes to him and begins to anoint the unconscious man, who even now seems to indicate some displeasure with the priest for conferring this sacrament. The question which these authors and many others propose is whether the sacrament is to be regarded as valid when conferred under such circumstances.

Authors agree that such an administration would be certainly valid.[9] Their conclusion is reached in a manner similar to that of the first example. There are here present, as Gobat pointed out,[10] two intentions. The first is the intention not to receive the sacrament of extreme unction, since he does not believe himself to be in danger of death. The second intention is to die in a Christian manner, and, therefore, to receive the sacraments of the Church before he dies.

The first intention is certainly present, since on several occasions he has given explicit expression to it. The presence of the second intention may be presumed simply from the fact that the man is a Catholic. His own personal conduct, however, makes

[8] *Elementa Theologiae Moralis,* (6. ed., Taurini, 1938), n. 110.

[9] Piscetta-Gennaro, *Elementa Theologiae Moralis,* V, n. 110; Noldin, *Summa Theologiae Moralis,* III, n. 41; Cappello, *De Sacramentis,* I, n. 75.

[10] *Opera Moralia,* Tr. 1, *de sacramentis in genere,* sect. vi, n. 226.

this fact certain, since he has spoken of his own reverence and respect for the sacrament of extreme unction. He has received the Eucharist several times during his illness. He has finally expressly indicated a desire to die in a Catholic manner. Hence there can be no doubt that, if he understood the danger of death in which he exists, he would most eagerly request the administration of extreme unction.

The two intentions, then, are not equally prized. The second intention, namely to receive the sacraments of the Church when he is in danger of death, is the predominant intention, the intention which would be preferred when the recipient becomes aware that the two contrary intentions cannot co-exist.[11] The first intention, namely not to receive extreme unction at this time, which is the product of an error of fact, is to be considered revoked by the more general intention. It is this general intention which will guarantee the valid administration of extreme unction to Titius.

> Titius habuerit intentionem saltem implicitam et habitualem, et per voluntatem generalem Christiane moriendi correxerit voluntatem contrariam ex errore provenientem.[12]

What has been said up to now holds true, of course, only when the contrary intentions exist at the same time; it is not implied that the two intentions must be elicited simultaneously; it is assumed, however, that both intentions must in some way still be in existence at the same time. They may exist in the nature of an actual, a virtual, or even of a habitual intention. The original intention must never have been previously revoked.

Even if one of the intentions remains only as a habitual intention, while the other is an actual intention, the same rule applies. It is always the predominant intention which prevails. Hence, if the habitual intention is the predominant intention, then it is the one which one must look to in determining the validity of the sacrament. In such a case the earlier intention may in a sense be said to revoke the intention which is only later elicited.

> Si inter voluntates contrarias una succedat alteri, posterior valet, nisi prior revocaverit (saltem virtualiter) omnem

[11] Pruemmer, *Manuale Theologiae Moralis,* III, n. 66.

[12] Piscetta-Gennaro, *Elementa Theologiae Moralis,* V, n. 110.

voluntatem subsequentem, tunc enim prior voluntas, modo expresse non revocetur, certe praevalet.[13]

C. Two Intentions of Equally Applicable Force

The recipient of the sacrament may, however, have several contrary intentions all of which he prizes equally. All of these intentions then would be of equal value and efficacy. In such a situation there would in truth be no predominant intention. There would then be no room for the application of the rule given earlier for the cases wherein contrary intentions are present, namely that the predomnant intention will always prevail.

In seeking to determine which of two contrary intentions prevails when both appear to be prized and harbored in like measure and manner, one must distinguish the case wherein the two equally prized intentions are elicited simultaneously from the case wherein they are elicited consecutively. If a person intends to receive the baptism instituted by Christ, but at the same time intends to exclude the baptism conferred by the Catholic Church, and these intentions are equally prized, so that one intention cannot be truly said to be more general and universal than the other, or so that one cannot be said to be subordinated to the other, then the baptism would have to be considered invalid. This is the judgment of Lacroix:

> Quod si utraque intentio aequaliter appretiaret suum objectum nec judicari posset utra praevaleat, dicendum esset sacramentum non fieri.[14]

In a similar situation De Lugo, though he inclined to the side of invalidity for such a sacrament, nevertheless seemed to display much reluctance with reference to any open and certain declaration for invalidity.

> Si utraque illa voluntas esset simul . . . et utrumque aequaliter et aeque affectus ad utrumque, putarem non fieri sacramentum.[15]

[13] St. Alphonsus, *Theologia Moralis,* Lib. VI, n. 24.

[14] *Theologia Moralis,* Lib. VI, n. 69.

[15] *De Sacramentis in Genere,* Disp. viii, n. 124.

In this case the sacrament is invalid because the recipient with his two intentions is intending something which is impossible.[16]

If, however, the contrary intentions are elicited consecutively, that is, if one succeeds the other in a sequence of time, then the intention which comes last in point of time will generally prevail over the earlier intention, since the later contrary intention is considered as revoking all earlier intentions.[17] At times, however, it may occur that the earlier intention continues in effect, and, as has been pointed out above, revokes in a sense the intention which follows.

> Si inter intentiones contrarias una succedat alteri, posterior solet valere, nisi tamen prior intentio annulaverit inde ab initio omnem aliam intentionem subsequentem; nam tunc non posterior sed prior intentio praevalet.[18]

[16] Lacroix, *Theologia Moralis,* Lib. VI, n. 69.

[17] St. Alphonsus, *Theologia Moralis,* Lib. VI, n. 24.

[18] Pruemmer, *Manuale Theologiae Moralis,* III, n. 66.

CHAPTER IX

COMPULSION DOES NOT NECESSARILY INVALIDATE THE SACRAMENTS

A. History Shows That at Times Compulsion Was Employed

Various cases of conscience have arisen in the history of the Church in regard to the effect of force and compulsion upon the intention of the recipient of the sacraments. These difficulties related in the main to three sacraments, baptism, holy orders and matrimony. Civil rulers had too frequently employed their military might to coerce their unwilling subjects to embrace Christianity. King Sisebut of the Visigoths (d. 621) had compelled the Jews in his kingdom to accept baptism. Charlemagne (768-814) had made a similar demand upon his Saxon subjects. With reference to holy orders there were also many occasions when moral pressure, sometimes even physical violence, was used with a view to imposing the reception of orders. Well known are the examples of St. Augustine, St. Ambrose, St. Basil, St. Gregory of Nazianz, and others.

B. Compulsion Does Not Prevent the Giving of True Consent

Accordingly one of the problems most frequently discussed among the commentators of the medieval period was the very practical question as to when the use of compulsion would so vitiate the intention of the recipient as to render the sacrament invalid.

1. Some Claimed Consent Was Not Necessary

According to Innocent III there were not lacking in his own time those who claimed that, even when there was a positive rejection and refusal of the reception of baptism, nevertheless the sacrament could still be validly conferred, though the grace of the sacrament would not be gained. This they held to be true also of holy orders and of other similar sacraments.

> Sunt nonnulli qui dicunt, quod sacramenta, quae per se sortiuntur effectum, ut baptismus et ordo ceteraque similia, non solum dormientibus et amentibus, sed invitis etiam et contradicentibus, etsi non quantum ad rem, quantum tamen ad characterem, conferuntur.[1]

2. This View Is Contrary to the Practice of the Church

In answer Innocent III first pointed out how this opinion was obviously opposed to the constant practice of the Church. Practically, such a view implied that men could be forced to enter the Church against their will. Certainly it was something utterly opposed to the unchanging tradition of the Church, namely, that men should not be compelled to embrace the faith against their will, and thus become subject to its jurisdiction.

> Verum id est religioni Christianae contrarium, ut semper invitus et penitus contradicens ad recipiendam et servandam Christianitatem aliquis compellatur.[2]

In support of his assertion the Pope quoted the IV Council of Toledo (633).

> De Iudaeis autem praecepit sancta synodus, nemini deinceps vim ad credendum inferre . . . non vi, sed libera arbitrii facultate ut convertantur suadendi sunt, non potius impellendi. Qui autem iampridem ad Christianitatem coacti sunt, quia iam constat eos sacramentis divinis associatos, et baptismi gratiam suscepisse . . . oportet, ut fidem, quam vi vel necessitate susceperint, tenere cogantur.[3]

He could have quoted as well his own predecessors Gregory the Great (590-604), writing to Paschasius, Bishop of Naples, in which letter he forbade the disturbance of the Jewish worship,[4] and Clement III (1187-1191).[5]

[1] C. 3, X, *de baptismo et eius effectu,* III, 42.

[2] C. 3, X, *de baptismo et eius effectu,* III, 42.

[3] C. 5, D. XLV.

[4] "Qui sincera intentione extraneos a Christiana religione ad fidem cupiunt rectam adducere, blandimentis debent non asperitatibus studere, ne quorum mentem reddita a plano ratio poterat provocare, pellat procul adversitas."—C. 3, D. XLV.

[5] "Statuimus ut nullus Christianus invitos vel nolentes Iudaeos ad baptismum per violentiam venire compellat. . . ."—C. 9, X, *de Iudaeis, Saracenis, et eorum servis,* V, 6.

C. A Distinction in Unwillingness Must Be Made

Innocent rejected this first opinion and then proceeded to accept and give his approval to the opinion of those who declared that in seeking to determine the validity of the sacraments conferred upon the unwilling one must first distinguish the various degrees of unwillingness which might be found among the recipients of the sacrament.

> Propter quod inter invitum et invitum, coactum et coactum, alii non absurde distinguunt. . . .[6]

Thus if the recipient of the sacrament has been subjected to either moral or physical compulsion, if he has been tortured or threatened, and he then, simply to avoid further molestation, agrees to receive baptism, such a one receives the sacrament validly according to the Pontiff, since he receives the sacramental character. Moreover, he is obliged to an observance and practice of his new Christian faith.

> Is qui terroribus atque suppliciis violenter attrahitur, et, ne detrimentum incurrat, baptismi suscipit sacramentum, talis quidem . . . characterem suscipit Christianitatis impressum et ipse tamquam conditionaliter volens, licet absolute non velit, cogendus est ad observantiam fidei Christianae.[7]

If, however, no consent at all was present, or if the recipient consistently and throughout opposed the reception of the sacrament, and yet, despite his protests, the sacramental ceremony was nevertheless performed, such a person clearly did not receive either the character or, even much less, the grace of the sacrament.

> Ille vero, qui numquam consentit, sed penitus contradicit nec rem, nec characterem suscipit sacramenti. . . .[8]

In the first example cited, wherein the recipient agreed to accept baptism as a means to avoid further injury or molestation, there was present what Innocent III called a conditional willingness (*conditionaliter volens*) to receive the sacrament. This conditional willingness was viewed as sufficient, the sacrament was validly received, and in consequence the recipient became bound

[6] C. 3, X, *de baptismo et eius effectu,* III, 42.

[7] C. 3, X, *de baptismo et eius effectu,* III, 42.

[8] *Loc. cit.*

to an observance of his faith. Thus a complete willingness (*absolute volens*) to receive the sacrament, though desirable, is not an essential requisite.

In the second example, the recipient was absolutely unwilling to receive baptism (*numquam consentit sed penitus contradicit*). In this case no grace was conferred, nor was the sacramental character effectively imprinted. The absolute unwillingness of the recipient unquestionably excluded these effects.

This solution of Innocent III was based upon a distinction drawn from the writings of St. Augustine, a distinction which in turn found its way into the *Decretum* of Gratian. St. Augustine gave the example of a man who had committed perjury in order to save his own life. He did not want to commit the sin; he wished only to save his life. Still, he had to be accounted guilty of the sin, since he willed to perform this one act by which he could save his life.[9]

Hence, in the mind of Innocent III, force and compulsion did not necessarily exclude the will's freedom for action, or its responsibility for this action. If the compulsion was of such a nature as to permit the will nevertheless to remain free and to consent to the reception of the sacrament, then the recipient was to be regarded as at least conditionally willing, and thus able to receive the sacrament validly.

D. This Distinction Was Followed in the Gloss and by the Decretalists

A similar distinction was employed in the Gloss and among the commentators, with this difference that the latter looked rather at the objectively existing force or compulsion which was employed, and then judged whether or not this was of such a nature as entirely to exclude the intention. Such a distinction had already been earlier adopted by Pope Alexander III (1159-1181) in regard to the sacrament of matrimony.[10] If the force em-

[9] "Non per ipsum appetit, ut falsum juret, sed ut falsum jurando vivat." —C. 1, C. XV, q. 1.

[10] "De muliere quae est invita tradita viro et detenta, quum inter vim et vim sit differentia. . . ."—C. 6, X, *de sponsalibus et matrimoniis*, IV, 1; JL, n. 14235.

ployed was of such a nature as utterly to exclude any and all freedom of action on the part of the recipient, this compulsion was known as absolute compulsion, *coactio absoluta;* as such it excluded the valid reception of the sacrament.[11] If, however, the compulsion was not such as to exclude an intention, it was called a conditional compulsion, *coactio conditionalis;* such a compulsion did not prevent the valid reception either of baptism or of holy orders.[12]

This distinction between absolute and conditional compulsion is found frequently, both in the Gloss and among the commentators. The Gloss to the *Liber Sextus* furnishes examples of both kinds of compulsion. If someone was baptized forcibly by being bound and then carried to a spring and there immersed in its waters, while the form of baptism was pronounced over him, such a baptism was invalid.

> Si quis baptizatus coacte quia per violentiam fuit portatus supra fontes et fuit immersus cum prolatione verborum, "Ego te baptizo etc," talis non recipit sacramentum baptismi.[13]

If, however, the force was only in the form of a conditional compulsion, as when the recipient consented to receive baptism because of a fear of death or out of a fear of bodily torture, then, despite the compulsion, there was still a valid reception of the sacrament.

> Si coactio esset conditionalis, puta propter metum mortis vel cruciatus corporis consensit ut baptizaretur, tunc enim licet fuerit coactus, tamen recipit sacramentum baptismi.[14]

The principle upon which this solution was based with reference to this question was thus given expression by the authors:

> "Coacta voluntas, voluntas est." [15]

[11] "Si fuerit absoluta coactio, nullus character imprimitur. . . ."—*Glossa Ord.* ad c. 5, D. XLV, s.v. *coacti sunt.*

[12] "Coactio conditionalis, de qua hic loquitur, non impedit sacramentum baptismi, nec etiam sacramentum ordinis."—*Loc. cit.*

[13] *Glossa Ord.* ad c. 13, *de haereticis,* V, 2, in VI°, s.v. *contra.*

[14] *Loc. cit.*

[15] *Ibid.,* s.v. *absolute.*

The same distinctions and conclusions are to be found among the Decretalists. Hostiensis, in discussing the question of the validity of the baptism of those who were baptized forcibly, declared that, if there was present only a conditional compulsion, the baptism was validly received. The recipient, therefore, could in the future be required to practice the faith. If, however, the compulsion was absolute, then no sacrament was received.[16] Panormitanus agreed with the solution set forth by Hostiensis.[17] He offered as a reason for this the fact that in absolute compulsion the recipient was utterly and completely passive in his status, while in conditional compulsion the person retained an active rôle.

> Vis praecisa impedit impressionem characteris, secus in conditionali. Ratio est quia primo casu potius dicitur quis pati quam agere.[18]

E. The More Recent Authors Continue to Employ the Distinction of Innocent III

Modern authors, in discussing this question, have often returned to and employed the distinction made use of first by Innocent III in the decretal *Maiores,* though they have somewhat varied the terminology they employ. All agree that if a sacramental ceremony is foisted upon the recipient when he strenuously resists, then the sacrament is not valid.

> Si baptismus (idem valet et de ordinatione) violenter, atque animo palam contrario suscipiatur, supradictus Pontifex Innocentius III eadem decretali *Maiores, de Baptismo,* distinctione utendum iudicat. Etenim eos, qui minis, ac terrore correpti violentiae cedunt, Baptismum, ut sibi consulant, suscipientes, ab iis distinguit, quibus, etiam vi illata, contradicentibus palam, et reluctantibus, hoc sacramentum per vim

[16] "Si conditionalis fuit coactio, characterem recipit et baptizatus est, et cogendus est fidem servare. Quia coacta voluntas, voluntas est. . . . Si vero coactio absoluta fuerit, nihil agitur nec character imprimitur."—*Summa Aurea,* Lib. III, tit. 42, n. 11.

[17] In this connection one should note that Panormitanus used the terms *vis praecisa* and *vis conditionalis* in the same sense as other authors had employed the terms *coactio absoluta* and *coactio conditionalis.*

[18] Lib. III, tit. 42, c. *Item queritur,* n. 3.

confertur. Decernitur autem in primo casu, non in secundo, Baptismatis imprimi characterem.[19]

F. The Intention Must Be an Act Consciously and Deliberately Elicited

1. Violence Precludes Sufficient Consent

In seeking to determine why the sacrament is invalid in the one case, but valid in the other, authors begin with an analysis of a voluntary act. A voluntary act is one which "is produced by the will with rational knowledge of and an inclination toward the object."[20] The human act, then, must proceed with consciousness and deliberation.

There may be present certain factors which will impede the exercise of the will. Some, as ignorance and concupiscence, will be intrinsic factors; others, as violence and fear, will be extrinsic factors. These latter are capable either of completely destroying or of limiting in part the free consent of the subject in the reception of the sacraments.

Violence is "the using of greater force than can be resisted to compel another to perform some action against his will."[21] Acts placed by the person when he is under such severe duress are therefore neither free nor voluntary.[22]

Hence, from this brief summary, one can quickly grasp the reason why authors agree that any sacraments which are received under such physical compulsion must be regarded as invalid. Violence which is too great to be resisted effectively precludes any consent on the part of the recipient. It has, however, been shown earlier that the consent of the recipient is essential to a valid reception of the sacrament. Thus this invalidity is not one which is the result of human positive law, but rather it follows from the very nature and essence of the sacraments as they were instituted by Christ. Though Coronata speaks only in regard to

[19] Benedictus XIV, ep. *Postremo mense,* 28 febr. 1747, n. 49—Fontes, n. 377.

[20] Slater, *A Manual of Moral Theology,* Vol. I (3. ed., New York, 1909), p. 22.

[21] Slater, *A Manual of Moral Theology,* I, 40.

[22] Iorio, *Theologia Moralis,* I, n. 39.

orders, yet his words are applicable to the other sacraments as well:

> Ordinatio hominis vi physica coacti et prorsus reluctantis, profecto non solum gravissime illicita sed etiam ex ipso iure divino manifeste irrita est, quia in casu deest intentio necessaria in candidato, ut per se patet.[23]

Sporer declared that the use of physical force in the conferring of baptism and confirmation would render those two sacraments invalid as well.

> Invalidum est sacramentum, si adultus sit omnino invitus et involuntarius simpliciter, animo et voluntate omnino repugnante per meram vim coactus, ut si per vim omnino reluctans quis baptizetur, confirmetur, ordinetur.[24]

2. Fear Does Not Preclude the Giving of Sufficient Consent

"Fear is a shrinking from impending evil."[25] Now, ordinarily acts which are performed under the influence of fear are nevertheless voluntary and free. Fear does not generally preclude freedom, so that however great the fear, short of absolute frenzy, a man is still responsible for his actions, at least to some extent. Under the same circumstances a man can give true, though reluctant, consent to receive the sacraments. If the circumstances were different, he might not give this consent, but, in his present condition, he does consent. Hence, though this is a reluctant consent, nevertheless it is a true consent, which will suffice for a valid, if not a licit, reception of the sacraments.

> Validum est sacramentum qui ex solo metu etiam gravi et injuste incusso suscipit: quia metus non tollit voluntarium simpliciter, sed tantum secundum quid: dummodo metu adactus velit suscipere sacramentum formaliter seu ea intentione quo Christus instituit et Ecclesia facit.[26]

[23] *De Sacramentis,* II, n. 61.

[24] *Theologia Moralis Sacramentalis,* Pars I, c. 2, sect. 3, n. 142.

[25] Davis, *Moral and Pastoral Theology,* Vol. I (5. ed., New York, Sheed and Ward, 1946), p. 27.

[26] Sporer, *Theologia Moralis Sacramentalis,* Pars I, c. 2, sect. 3, n. 143.

G. The Code Confirms This Teaching

Confirmation for this view can be found in canon 214, § 1. The canon deals with the case of a cleric who has been compelled to receive one of the sacred orders under duress. It outlines the procedure which the competent authorities must observe in determining whether this cleric is bound by the clerical obligations which accompany this order. There is no question that the cleric has validly received the order.[27]

Some authors regard the hindrance of *vis vel metus gravis* with reference to a valid marriage as a hindrance which derives from the very law of nature.[28] They argue that the existence of such a hindrance is acknowledged as necessary because of the perpetual and indissoluble bond which is created between the parties as well as in view of the serious inseparable obligations which accompany the married state. Cappello offers the objection that certainly all will concede that the obligations of the clerical state are of even greater import. Hence, he reasons, should it not also be said that an order received under grave fear should likewise be regarded as invalid? [29]

Cappello answers his own objection when he points out that this line of argumentation abstracts from the fact that the obligations of the married state arise from the very nature of the marriage contract. The obligations connected with the priestly state, on the other hand, are annexed to it by purely positive ecclesiastical law. Thus, though it might occur that the sacrament of orders was validly received, it is not a necessary consequence that the obligations which normally accompany the order were also effectively assumed.[30]

[27] "Clericus, qui metu gravi coactus ordinem sacrum recepit. . . ."—canon 214, § 1.

[28] Canon 1087.

[29] *De Sacramentis,* IV, n. 359.

[30] *Loc. cit.*

CONCLUSIONS

1. Infants and the perpetually insane are capable of receiving baptism, confirmation, Holy Eucharist, and holy orders; they are incapable of receiving penance and extreme unction.

2. The intention for infants and the perpetually insane is supplied by Christ and by the Church.

3. An intention is required for adults for the valid reception of the sacraments.

4. A habitual intention is required but also suffices for the valid reception of the sacraments, including penance.

5. Resistance on the part of the insane to the reception of the sacraments is not to be regarded as a revocation of the earlier intention of receiving them, since such a revocation, like the eliciting of the intention itself, must flow from a human act.

6. A sufficient implicit intention for baptism is contained in the desire to become a Christian, even though there is no awareness of the existence and necessity of the sacrament.

7. Though it seems that an implicit intention for baptism is not contained in an act of supernatural attrition, yet the contrary opinion must be accounted to have at least extrinsic probability, and should be followed in practice in the presence of one who is in danger of death.

8. The desire to live and die as a Catholic contains a sufficient implicit intention for the reception of confirmation, Holy Viaticum, extreme unction, and penance, at least in cases of extreme necessity.

9. For the reception of the Eucharist outside the case of Viaticum an explicit habitual intention is probably required.

10. The Code provides that obstinate impenitence is to be regarded as indicating the absence of a sufficient intention for the reception of extreme unction.

11. Though inherently an implicit intention is sufficient for all the sacraments, it is difficult to uncover a general intention so broad as to contain an implicit intention for the reception of holy orders.

12. The general intention to live and die as a Catholic does not constitute a sufficient intention for the reception of the sacraments by those who are temporarily without the use of their senses, e.g., by those who are asleep, drunk, etc.

13. An internal intention is required for the validity of the sacraments, and the contrary opinion of Gasparri is to be regarded as having no probability at all.

14. When two contrary intentions are present in the same subject, then the predominant intention will alone prevail.

15. Not all compulsion renders the reception of the sacraments invalid, but only that in the face of which the subject is completely unwilling (*absolute nolens*).

BIBLIOGRAPHY

Sources

Benedictus XIV, *Benedicti XIV Ponti. Opt. Max. Bullarium, in quo continentur Constitutiones, Epistolae, etc. editae ab initio Pontificatus usque ad annum 1746,* Prati, 1845.

Bouscaren, T. Lincoln, *The Canon Law Digest,* 3 vols. and Supplements through 1955, Milwaukee: Bruce, 1934—1949—1953—1954—1955—1956.

Codex Iuris Canonici, Pii X Pontificis Maximi iussu digestus, Benedicti Papae XV auctoritate promulgatus, Praefatione, Fontium Annotatione et Indice Analytico-Alphabetico, ab Emo Petri Card. Gasparri Auctus, Romae: Typis Polyglottis Vaticanis, 1917.

Codicis Iuris Canonici Fontes, cura Emi Petri Card. Gasparri editi, 9 vols., Romae (postea Civitate Vaticana): Typis Polyglottis Vaticanis, 1923-1939 (Vols. VII-IX, ed. cura et studio Emi Iustiniani Car. Serédi).

Corpus Iuris Canonici, editio Lipsiensis Secunda, post Aemilii Richteri curas instruxit Aemilius Friedberg, 2 vols., Lipsiae, 1879-81.

Decretales D. Gregorii Papae IX, una cum Glossis Restitutae, Romae, 1582.

Decretum Gratiani Emendatum et Notationibus Illustratum una cum Glossis, Gregorii XIII Ponti. Max. iussu editum, 2 vols., Romae, 1582.

Liber Sextus Decretalium D. Bonifacii Pape VIII, Suae Integritati una cum Clementinis et Extravagantibus, Earumque Glossis Restitutus, Romae, 1582.

Jaffé, Phillipus, *Regesta Pontificum Romanorum ab condita ecclesia ad annum post Christum natum 1198, editionem 2. correctam et auctam auspiciis Gulielmi Wattenbach curaverunt F. Kaltenbrunner, P. Ewald, S. Loewenfeld,* 2 vols., Lipsiae, 1885-1888.

Mansi, Ioannes, *Sacrorum Conciliorum Nova et Amplissima Collectio,* 53 vols. in 59, Paris-Arnhem-Leipzig, 1901-1927.

Potthast, Augustus, *Regesta Pontificum Romanorum inde ab anno post Christum natum 1198 ad annum 1304,* 2 vols., Berolini, 1874-75.

Rituale Romanum, Pauli V Pontificis Maximi iussu editum aliorumque Pontificum cura recognitum atque auctoritate SSmi D. N. Pii Papae XI ad normam Codicis Iuris Canonici accommodatum, 3. ed., New York, 1947.

Schroeder, H. J., *Canons and Decrees of the Council of Trent,* St. Louis: Herder, 1941.

Reference Works

Abbo, John-Hannan, Jerome, *The Sacred Canons,* 2 vols., St. Louis: Herder, 1952.

Aquinas, St. Thomas, *Summa Theologiae,* 5 vols., Matriti: Biblioteca de Autores Cristianos, 1952.

Benedictus XIV, *De Synodo Dioecesana,* 2 vols., Romae, 1748.

———, *Commentarius de Sacrosancto Missae Sacrificio,* Tom. II, Lovanii, 1762.

Bennington, J. C., *The Subject of Confirmation,* The Catholic University of America Canon Law Studies, n. 267, Washington, D. C.: The Catholic University of America Press, 1952.

Billot, Ludovicus, *De Ecclesiae Sacramentis,* 7. ed., 2 vols., Romae, 1931.

Billuart, Carolus, *Summa Sancti Thomae,* 8 vols., Parisiis, n.d.

Blat, Albert, *Commentarium Textus Codicis Iuris Canonici,* Lib. III, 1, 2. ed., Romae, 1924.

Boich, Henricus, *In Quinque Decretalium Libros Commentaria,* Venetiis, 1576.

Bonacina, Martinus, *Opera Omnia,* 3 vols., Venetiis, 1687.

Bucceroni, Ianuarius, *Institutiones Theologiae Moralis,* 6. ed., 3 vols., Romae, 1915.

Connell, Franciscus, *De Sacramentis Ecclesiae,* New York: Pustet, 1923.

Cappello, Felix, *De Sacramentis,* 5 vols., Vol. I, 5. ed., Romae: Marietti, 1947; Vol. II, 5. ed., 1947; Vol. III, 3. ed., 1949; Vol. IV, 2. ed., 1947.

Coronata, Matthaeus Conte a, *De Sacramentis,* Vol. I, 2. ed., 1951; Vol. II, 2. ed., 1949, Taurini: Marietti.

Davis, H., *Moral and Pastoral Theology,* Vol. I, 5. ed., New York: Sheed and Ward, 1946.

De Lugo, Ioannes, *Disputationes Scholasticae et Morales,* 8 vols., Parisiis, 1868-1869.

Doronzo, E., *De Sacramentis in Genere,* Milwaukee: Bruce, 1946.

Ferraris, Lucius, *Bibliotheca Canonica, Iuridica, Moralis, Theologica, necnon Ascetica, Polemica, Rubricistica, Historica,* 9 vols., Romae, 1885-1899.

Gasparri, Petrus, *Tractatus Canonicus de Sacra Ordinatione,* 2 vols., Parisiis, 1893.

Genicot, Eduardus–Salsmans, Josephus, *Institutiones Theologiae Moralis,* 14. ed., 2 vols., Buenos Aires: Desclée, 1943.

Gilson, E., *The Christian Philosophy of St. Thomas Aquinas,* New York: Random House, 1956.

Gobat, Georgius, *Opera Moralia,* 2 vols., Venetiis, 1749.

Hostiensis, Cardinalis (Henricus de Segusio), *Summa Aurea,* Venetiis, 1570.

Innocentius IV, *In Quinque Libros Decretalium Commentaria,* Venetiis, 1570.

Ioannes Andreae, *In Tertium Librum Decretalium Novella Commentaria,* Venetiis, 1581.

Iorio, Thomas, *Theologia Moralis,* 4. ed., 3 vols., Neapoli: D'Auria, 1953-1954.

Kilker, Adrian, *Extreme Unction,* The Catholic University of America Canon Law Studies, n. 32, Washington, D. C.: The Catholic University of America, 1926.

King, James, *The Administration of the Sacraments to Dying Non-Catholics,* The Catholic University of America Canon Law Studies, n. 23, Washington, D. C.: The Catholic University of America, 1924.

Lacroix, Claudius, *Theologia Moralis,* 2 vols., Coloniae, 1719.

Lanza, Antonius, *Theologia Moralis,* Vol. I, Taurini-Romae: Marietti, 1949.

Laymann, Paulus, *Theologia Moralis,* 2 vols., Bambergae, 1669.

Leeming, Bernard, *Principles of Sacramental Theology,* Westminster, Md.: Newman, 1956.

Lehmkuhl, Augustinus, *Theologia Moralis,* Vol. II, 9. ed., Friburgi Brisgoviae, 1898.

Lennerz, H., *De Sacramento Baptismi,* 2. ed., Romae, 1948.

Liguori, St. Alphonsus, *Theologia Moralis,* ed. L. Gaudé, 4 vols., Romae, 1905-1912.

Many, S., *Praelectiones de Sacra Ordinatione,* Parisiis, 1905.

Merkelbach, *Summa Theologiae Moralis,* 8. ed., 3 vols., Montréal: Desclée, 1949.

Migne, J. P., *Patrologiae Cursus Completus,* Series Latina, 221 vols., Paris, 1844-64.

Noldin, H.-Schmitt, A., *Summa Theologiae Moralis,* 27. ed., 3 vols., Oeniponte-Lipsiae: Rauch, 1940.

Panormitanus, Abbas, *Commentaria in Quinque Libros Decretalium,* 5 vols. in 7, Venetiis, 1588.

Piscetta, A.-Gennaro, A., *Elementa Theologiae Moralis,* Vol. V, 6. ed., Taurini, 1938.

Pruemmer, Dominicus, *Manuale Theologiae Moralis,* 12. ed., edited by E. Muench, Friburgi Brisgoviae–Barcinone: Herder, 1955.

Slater, Thomas, *A Manual of Moral Theology,* Vol. I, 3. ed., New York, 1909.

Sporer, Patritius, *Theologia Moralis Sacramentalis,* 3. ed., Salisburgi, 1711.

Statkus, Francis, *The Minister of the Last Sacraments,* The Catholic University of America Canon Law Studies, n. 299, Washington, D. C.: The Catholic University of America Press, 1951.

Suarez, Franciscus, *Commentarius et Disputationes in Tertiam Partem D. Thomae,* Vivès ed. (*Opera Omnia,* Tom. XX), Parisiis, 1860.

Tanquerey, Ad., *Synopsis Theologiae Dogmaticae,* 24. ed., 3 vols., New York: Benziger, 1938.

Tournely, Honoratus, *Praelectiones Theologicae de Sacramentis in genere quas in scholis sorbonicis habuit,* Parisiis, 1726.

Vazquez, Gabriel, *Commentarium ac Disputationum in Tertiam Partem Sancti Thomae Tomus II,* Lugduni, 1631.

Vermeersch, Arthur, *Theologia Moralis,* 4. ed., 4 vols., Romae: Pontificia Universita Gregoriana, 1948.

Vermeersch, A.-Creusen, I, *Epitome Iuris Canonici,* 3 vols., Vol. II, 7. ed., Mechlinae-Romae: Dessain, 1954.

Waldron, Joseph, *The Minister of Baptism,* The Catholic University of America Canon Law Studies, n. 170, Washington, D. C.: The Catholic University of America Press, 1942.

Wernz, F.-Vidal, P., *Ius Canonicum,* Tom. IV, 1, Romae, 1934.

Zeiger, Ivo, *Historia Iuris Canonici,* 2 vols., Romae: Apud Aedes Universitatis Gregorianae, 1947.

Articles

McCarthy, John, *Irish Ecclesiastical Record,* 5. Series, LXVI (1945), 369.

Pruemmer, Dominicus, "The Recipient of Extreme Unction According to the Code," *The Homiletic and Pastoral Review,* XXVI (1926), 740-741.

Umberg, Ioannes, "De Reviviscentia Sacramentorum Ratione Rei et Sacramenti," *Periodica,* XVII (1928), 22*-23*.

Vermeersch, Arthur, "Practica disquisitio de sacramentis conferendis vel negandis acatholico," *Periodica,* XVIII (1929), 129*.

Periodicals

Homiletic and Pastoral Review, The, New York, 1900—(1900-1917: *Homiletic Monthly and Catechist;* 1917-1918; *Homiletic Monthly;* 1918-1920: *Homiletic Monthly and Pastoral Review*).

Irish Ecclesiastical Record, The, Dublin, 1864—

Periodica de Religiosis et Missionariis, Brugis, 1905-1919; ab anno 1920; *Periodica de Re Canonica et Morali, utilia praesertim Religiosis et Missionariis,* Brugis, 1920-1927; *Periodica de Re Morali, Canonica, Liturgica,* Brugis, 1927-1936, et Romae, 1937—

INDEX

BIOGRAPHICAL NOTE

Leo Vincent Vanyo was born on October 18, 1925, in Munhall, Pennsylvania. He received his elementary and high school education in the Munhall Public Schools. After graduation from Munhall High School in 1943, he entered the Pontifical College Josephinum at Worthington, Ohio. He was ordained to the priesthood at the Josephinum on June 7, 1952. He taught History, Latin, and Greek at the Josephinum from 1952 until May, 1954. In September of 1954 he entered the School of Canon Law of the Catholic University of America, where he received the degree of the Baccalaureate in Canon Law in June, 1955, and the degree of the Licentiate in Canon Law in June, 1956.

CANON LAW STUDIES *

No. 375. Kelleher, Rev. Francis T., A.B., J.C.L., Judicial expenses.

No. 376. Bantigue, Rev. Pedro N., J.C.L., The Provincial Council of Manila of 1771.
(Its text followed by a commentary on *Actio II, De Episcopis*).

No. 377. Burns, Rev. Dennis J., J.C.L., Matrimonial indissolubility: contrary conditions.

No. 378. Deutsch, Rev. Bernard F., J.C.L., Jurisdiction of pastors in the external forum.

No. 379. Dunnivan, Rev. John P., A.B., J.C.L., Prejudicial attempts in pending litigation.

No. 380. Ernst, Rev. Albert C., A.B., J.C.L., Free admission to the church for sacred rites.

No. 381. Frattin, Peter Louis, J.C.L., The matrimonial impediment of impotence: occlusion of the spermatic ducts and vaginismus.

No. 382. Henry, Rev. Charles W., O.S.B., A.B., S.T.L., J.C.L., Canonical relations between bishops and abbots at the beginning of the tenth century.

No. 383. Hoffman, Rev. Lawrence J., A.B., S.T.B., J.C.L., Clergy Conferences: Canon 131.

No. 384. Markham, Rev. James J., A.B., S.T.L., J.C.L., The Sacred Congregation of Seminaries and Universities of Studies.

No. 385. McGrath, Rev. John J., A.B., LL.B., J.C.L., A comparative study of crime and its imputability in ecclesiastical criminal law and in American criminal law.

No. 386. McGuire, Rev. James D., O.R.S.A., J.C.L., The postulancy.

No. 387. Munday, Rev. James E., J.C.L., Ecclesiastical Property in Australia and New Zealand.

No. 388. Murphy, Rev. Joseph P., A.B., J.C.L., The laws of the State of New York affecting church property.

No. 389. Pickard, Rev. Wm. M., J.C.L., Judicial experts: a source of evidence in ecclesiastical trials.

No. 390. Ruddy, Rev. James, J.C.L., The Apostolic Constitution *Christus Dominus:* text, translation and commentary, with short annotations on the Motu Proprio *Sacram Communionem.*

No. 391. Vanyo, Rev. Leo V., A.B., J.C.L., Requisites of intention in the reception of the sacraments.

www.ingramcontent.com/pod-product-compliance
Lightning Source LLC
LaVergne TN
LVHW050208080826
844660LV00012B/382

* 9 7 8 0 8 1 3 2 2 5 5 1 7 *